The Wicked Book

of

JOKES FOR
COOL KIDS

The Wicked Book

of

JOKES FOR
COOL KIDS

$\boxed{p}$

This is a Parragon Book
This edition published in 2002

Parragon
Queen Street House
4 Queen Street
Bath BA1 1HE, UK

Produced by Magpie Books, an imprint of
Constable & Robinson Ltd. London

Copyright © Parragon 2001

ISBN 0-75259-384-6

A copy of the British Library Cataloguing-in-Publication Data
is available from the British Library

Printed and bound in Italy

Contents

Summer
Sensations

Where does an elephant go on holiday?
Tuscany.

What do you call a mosquito on holiday?
An itch-hiker.

What do you say to a hitch-hiking frog?
"Hop in!"

What do you get if you cross a frog with a ferry?
A hoppercraft.

How do toads travel?
By hoppercraft.

Which Cornish town is the favorite holiday spot for rodents?
Mousehole.

What do bees do if they want to use public transport?
Wait at a buzz stop.

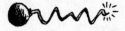

What happened when the cannibal crossed the Atlantic on the QE2?
He told the waiter to take the menu away and bring him the passenger list.

Where do witches go for their holidays?
Bat-lins.

Where did vampires go to first in
America?
New-fang-land.

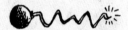

Where do Chinese vampires come from?
Fanghai.

Where do zombies go for cruises?
The Deaditerranean.

What do demons have on holiday?
A devil of a time.

Where do ghosts go on holiday?
The Ghosta Brava.

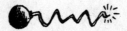

Where do ghost trains stop?
At devil crossings.

Why are ghosts at their loudest in
August?
Because they're on their howlidays.

Which airway do ghouls fly with?
British Scareways.

Where do ghosts like to go on holiday?
Goole.

How did the rabbit get to Australia?
He flew by hareplane.

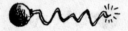

James: Do you know what nice people do on holiday?
John: No.
James: I didn't think you would.

Why couldn't the skeleton pay his bus fare?
Because he was skint.

Why did the bat miss the bus?
Because he hung around too long.

Why do you have to wait so long for a ghost train to come along?
They only run a skeleton service.

1st ghost: I died at Waterloo, you know.
2nd ghost: Really? Which platform?

1st witch: I'm going to France tomorrow.
2nd witch: Are you going by broom?
1st witch: No, by hoovercraft.

Did you hear about the ghost who learned to fly?
He was pleased to be back on terror-firma.

Where do ants go for their holidays?
Fr-ants.

How do fleas travel?
Itch-hiking.

What steps should you take if you see a dangerous yeti on your travels?
Very large ones.

What do Paddington Bear and Winnie the Pooh pack for their holidays?
The bear essentials.

The seaside resort we went to last year was so boring that one day the tide went out and never came back.

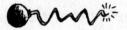

My girlfriend talks so much that when she goes on holiday, she has to spread suntan lotion on her tongue.

Boss: You're looking much better now, Reynolds. How's that pain?
Reynolds: She's away on a business trip.

Charlie was very nervous about going in a plane. "Do these planes crash often?" he asked the flight attendant.
"No," she smiled, "only once."

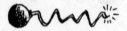

Nellie: Our teacher went to the West Indies for her holidays.
Kelly: Jamaica?
Nellie: No, she went of her own accord.

What can you see from the top of the
Eiffel Tower?
Quite an eyeful!

Which American city would a cow like to
visit?
Moo York.

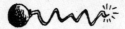

Crossing the Atlantic in a Rowing Boat – by
Eva Lott

Summertime – by Theresa Greene

What did the sea say to the beach?
Nothing, it just waved.

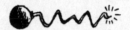

Sarah: I'm going to sunbathe on my holiday. I love the sun.
Susie: Oh, so do I. I could lie in the sun all day and all night.

Darren went on a camping holiday with his family. "Did the tent leak?" asked his friend Sharon.
"Only when it rained," answered Darren.

Why did the principal like to take her main holiday in the spring?
She liked clean sheets on her bed.

Lizzie got a bad case of sunburn. When she complained how sore it was, her brother remarked, "Well, I guess you basked for it."

Passenger: Does this bus go to London?
Bus driver: No.
Passenger: But it says London on the front.
Bus driver: It says fish fingers on the side but we don't sell them!

In the summer holidays the math teacher collected information for a national opinion poll. But after a week she was sacked. Her vital statistics were wrong.

Mrs Broadbeam: Now, remember, children, travel is very good for you. It broadens the mind.
Sarah, muttering: If you're anything to go by, that's not all it broadens!

Pattie: We had a burglary last night, and they took everything except the soap and towels.

Peter: The dirty crooks.

A pilot flying over the jungle was having trouble with his plane and decided to bail out before it crashed. So he got into his parachute, jumped, pulled the rip-cord, and drifted gently down to land. Unfortunately he landed right in a large cooking pot which a tribal chief was simmering gently over a fire. The chief looked at him, rubbed his eyes, looked again, and asked, "What's this flier doing in my soup?"

After years of traveling around the world in his search, the wicked Abanazar finally discovered the enchanted cave in which he believed lay the magic lamp which would make him millions. He stood before the boulders which sealed the cave, and uttered the magic words, "Open, sesame!" There was a silence, and then a ghostly voice from within moaned, "Open says-a-who?"

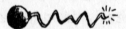

Why did the stupid pilot land his plane on a house?
Because the landing lights were on.

Harry was telling his friend about his holiday in Switzerland. His friend had never been to Switzerland, and asked, "What did you think of the scenery?"
"Oh, I couldn't see much," Harry admitted. "There were all those mountains in the way."

"Why did you come back early from your holidays?" one of Alec's friends asked him.
"Well, on the first day we were there one of the chickens died and that night we had chicken soup. The next day one of the pigs died and we had pork chops . . ."
"But why did you come back?"
"Well, on the third day the farmer's father-in-law died. What would you have done?"

What's green, has four legs and two trunks?
Two seasick tourists.

A woman just back from the United States was telling her friends about the trip.
"When my husband first saw the Grand Canyon, his face dropped a mile," she said.
"Why, was he disappointed with the view?"
"No, he fell over the edge."

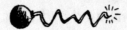

What is the best thing to take into the desert?
A thirst-aid kit.

A new porter at a Paris hotel was instructed by the manager that it was important to call the guests by their names, in order to make them feel welcome and that the easiest way to find out their name was to look at their luggage. Armed with this advice, the porter took two guests up to their rooms, put down their bags and said, "I hope you 'ave a very 'appy stay 'ere in Paris, Mr and Mrs Genuine Cow'ide."

What do you think of this suit? I had it made in Hong Kong.
Very nice, but what's that hump on the back?
Oh, that's the tailor. He's still working on it.

"I hope this plane doesn't travel faster than sound," said the old lady to the flight attendant.

"Why?"

"Because my friend and I want to talk, that's why."

Last time my wife and I traveled on the ferry from Newhaven to Dieppe, we had six meals.

Six meals for that short crossing?

Three down and three up.

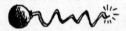

A naughty child was irritating all the passengers on the flight from London to New York. At last one man could stand it no longer. "Hey kid," he shouted, "Why don't you go outside and play?"

The transatlantic liner was experiencing particularly heavy weather, and Mrs Ramsbottom wasn't feeling well.
"Would you care for some more supper, madam?" asked the steward.
"No thanks," replied the wretched passenger. "Just throw it overboard to save me the trouble."

First explorer: There's one thing about
Jenkinson.
Second explorer: What's that?
First explorer: He could go to
headhunters' country without any fear –
they'd have no interest in him.

Why is it not safe to sleep on trains?
Because they run over sleepers.

What is red outside, green and hairy
inside, and very crowded?
A bus full of gooseberries.

What's green and hairy and wears sunglasses?
A gooseberry on holiday.

What's sweet, sour, dangerous and travels?
Takeaway Kung food.

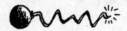

Where's a shark's favorite holiday destination?
Finland.

How do nits go on holidays?
British Hairways.

Why won't midfield players travel by airplane?
In case they are put on the wing.

What's red and wobbles on top of sponge cake and custard in the middle of Paris?
The Trifle Tower.

What makes the Tower of Pisa lean?
It doesn't eat much.

Kylie and Riley were talking about their forthcoming summer holidays. "Last year," said Kylie, "my brother and I took turns to bury each other in the sand."

"Yes, but what about this year?" interrupted Riley.

"I was coming to that," said Kylie. "This year we're going back to try to find him."

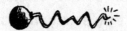

Local: Are you lost?
Stranger: No, I'm here. It's the bus station that's lost.

Letter from a travel agent: The flight you requested is fully booked but if someone falls out we'll let you know.

Notice at a railroad station: These toilets are out of order. Please use platform 6.

Louise: Did you hear about the stupid hitch-hiker?
Liza: No, what did he do?
Louise: He started his journey early so there wouldn't be so much traffic about.

Older brother: When I was a sailor I sailed both ways across the Atlantic without taking a bath.
Younger brother: I always said you were a dirty double crosser!

My Uncle Ben and Aunt Flo haven't had a row for five years.
That's wonderful.
Not really. Uncle Ben lives in China.

What happens when a plane runs out of fuel?
All the passengers get out to push.

Super
Slanders

What happens if you eat too much candy?
You take up two seats on the bus!

The school had given a concert and
Mrs Feather's son had played the piano.
She was very proud of him. She asked his
music teacher, "Do you think my Freddie
should take up the piano as a career?"
"No," replied the music teacher, "I think
he should put down the lid as a favor."

Ben's sister, Samantha, wanted to be an
actress when she left school.
"Is she pretty?" asked Bill.
"Let's just say she has a perfect face for
radio," answered Ben.

Nellie: I have an open mind.
Kelly: Yes, there's nothing in it.

Brian: How long can someone live without a brain?
Ryan: How old are you?

Lyn: I don't like soup.
Brian: I expect you can't get it to stay on the fork.

Trixie: When I die I'm going to leave my brain to science.
Tracey: I suppose every little helps.

Mick: Tim's gone to live in the city.
Nick: Why's that?
Mick: He'd read in the papers that the country was at war.

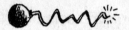

Man in clothes store: I'd like a blue shirt to match my eyes, please.
Sales clerk: I'm sorry, sir, we don't have any blue shirts. But we do have some soft hats that would match your head.

Jane: Do you ever do any gardening?
Wayne: Not often. Why?
Jane: You look as if you could do with some remedial weeding.

Jen: You look as if you'd find it hard to chew gum and walk at the same time.
Ken: And you look as if you'd find it hard to chew gum and breathe at the same time!

Barry: You're like uncultivated woodland.
Gary: Really?
Barry: Yes, totally dense.

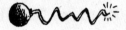

Did you hear about the boy who was known as Fog?
He was thick and wet.

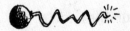

Holly: Do you ever find life boring?
Dolly: I didn't until I met you.

He's so stupid he thinks a cucumber is something you play pool with.

She's so stupid she thinks Christmas Eve is a tug of war.

Charlie: Do you think I'm intelligent?
Chrissie: I'd like to say "yes" but my Mom says I must always tell the truth.

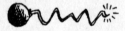

Emma: I'd like to say something nice about you as it's your birthday.
Gemma: Why don't you?
Emma: Because I can't think of a single thing to say!

Ivan: They say Ian has a dual personality.
Ivor: Let's hope the other one is brighter than this one!

Madge: Your body's quite well organized.
Martin: How do you mean?
Madge: The weakest part – your brain – is protected by the strongest – your thick skull!

Suresh: Whatever will Clive do when he leaves school? I can't see him being bright enough to get a job.
Sandra: He could always be a ventriloquist's dummy.

Hazel: I wonder what my IQ is?
Heather: Don't worry about it, it's nothing.

I always like to think the best of people,
that's why I think of you as a complete
idiot.

She has a mind of her own.
Of course she does. No one else would
want it.

Did you hear someone has invented a coffin
that just covers the head? It's for people
like you who're dead from the neck up!

Bertie: You remind me of a Greek statue.
Gertie: Do you mean you think I'm beautiful?
Bertie: Yes, beautiful, but not all there.

Bennie: I've been told I must lose 5 kg of surplus fat.
Kenny: You could always cut off your head.

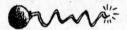

Cary: There's no point in telling you a joke with a double meaning.
Mary: Why not?
Cary: You wouldn't get either of them.

I'd like you to accept my opinion for what it's worth.
That means you owe me one cent.

My brother said he'd tell me everything he knows.
He must have been speechless.

Stella: Tracey has a ready wit.
Sheila: Perhaps she could let us know when it's ready!

Daniel: Being clever isn't everything.
Denzil: In your case it isn't anything.

My sister's going out with David.
Any girl who goes out with David must be able to appreciate the simpler things in life.

They say Margaret is a raving beauty.
You mean she's escaped from a loony bin?

In one way Julian is lucky. If he went out of his mind no one would notice the difference.

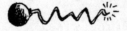

I feel sorry for your little mind – all alone in that great big head.

Jonathan ought to be a boxer. Someone might knock him conscious.

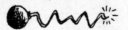

Why is your brother always flying off the handle?
Because he's got a screw loose.

Marie: Two heads are better than one.
Gary: In your case none might be better than one!

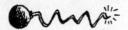

His speech started at 2 p.m. sharp.
And finished at 3 p.m. dull.

They call him Baby-face.
Does that mean he has a brain to match?

Brian: Let's play a game of wits.
Diane: No, Let's play something you can play too.

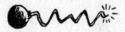

They say many doctors have examined her brain – but they can't find anything in it.

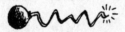

Don't let your mind wander. It's not strong enough to be allowed out on its own.

Jane: Do you like me?
Wayne: As girls go, you're fine. And the sooner you go the better!

Handsome Harry: Every time I walk past a girl she sighs.
Wisecracking William: With relief!

Freda: Boys whisper they love me.
Fred: Well, they wouldn't admit it out loud, would they?

Jerry: Is that a new perfume I smell?
Kerry: It is, and you do!

Laura: Whenever I go to my local shop the shopkeeper shakes my hand.

Lionel: I expect it's to make sure you don't put it in his till.

Bernie: Why have you given me this piece of rope?

Ernie: They say if you give someone enough rope they'll hang themselves!

Peter: My brother wants to work badly.

Anita: As I remember, he usually does.

Michael: It's hard for my sister to eat.

Maureen: Why?

Michael: She can't bear to stop talking.

Boss: Are you willing to do an honest day's work?
Secretary: Yes, as long as you give me an honest week's pay for it.

Son: How old are you, Dad?
Dad: Oh, around 35.
Son: I expect you've been around it a few times!

My brother's looking for a wife.
Trouble is, he can't find a woman who loves him as much as he loves himself.

He reminds me of a bowl of custard.
Yes, yellow and thick.

They say he works eight hours and sleeps eight hours.
Problem is, they're the same eight hours.

My dad once stopped a man ill-treating a donkey.
It was a case of brotherly love.

Gordon: My wallet's full of big bills.
Graham: All unpaid, I expect.

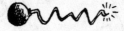

Jimmy: Is that lemonade OK?
Timmy: Yes. Why do you ask?
Jimmy: I just wondered if it was as sour as your face.

Lee: Our family's descended from royalty.
Dee: King Kong?

Anne: Do you think I look awful in this dress?
Dan: You could look worse – if I had better eyesight!

Mary: Do you think my sister's pretty?
Gary: Well, Let's just say if you pulled her pigtail she'd probably say "oink, oink."

Cheryl: They say I have an infectious laugh.
Meryl: In that case don't laugh near me!

Do you like my new baby sister? The stork brought her.
Hmm, it looks as if the stork dropped her on her head.

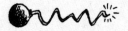

My sister went on a crash diet.
Is that why she looks a wreck?

My brother's on a seafood diet.
Really?
Yes, the more he sees food the more he eats.

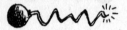

Penny: No one could call your dad a quitter.
Kenny: No, he's been sacked from every job he's ever had.

Terry: When my mother was young she had a coming-out party.
Gerry: When they saw her they probably sent her back in again.

Winnie: I was cut out to be a genius.
Ginny: Pity no one put the pieces together properly.

I hear she was a war baby.
I'm not surprised – I expect her parents took one look at her and started fighting.

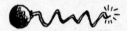

Does he have a big mouth?
Put it this way, he can sing a duet by himself.

Roy: They say ignorance is bliss.
Rita: Then you should be the happiest boy in the world.

Does your brother keep himself clean?
Oh, yes. He takes a bath every month
whether he needs one or not.

His left eye must be fascinating.
Why do you say that?
Because his right eye looks at it all the
time.

How can she be so fat? She eats like a
bird!
Yes, a vulture!

She once had a million-dollar figure.
Trouble is, inflation set in.

My boyfriend only has two faults –
everything he says and everything he does!

I hear he's a very careful person.
Well, he likes to economize on soap and
water.

That girl looks like Helen Black.
She looks even worse in white.

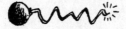

Rich lady: That painting you did of me
doesn't do me justice.
Artist: It's not justice you want, it's
mercy!

New wife: Will you love me when I'm old and fat and ugly?
New husband: Of course I do!

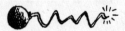

She's so ugly that when a wasp stings her it shuts its eyes.

Bill and Gill make a perfect pair, don't they?
They certainly do. She's a pill and he's a headache.

They say she has a sharp tongue.
Yes, she can slice bread with it.

They say cleanliness is next to godliness.
With some people it's next to impossible!

Does he tell lies?
Let's just say his memory exaggerates.

Jane: I'll cook dinner. What would you like?
Shane: Good life insurance.

Harry's very good for other people's health.
Whenever they see him coming they go for a long walk!

Did you say he had a big mouth?
Put it this way, he's the only person I know
who can eat a banana sideways!

She could give a headache to an aspirin!

He's watching his weight.
Yes, watching it go up!

He's a light eater.
Yes, as soon as it's light he starts eating!

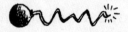

The last time I saw a face like yours I
threw it a banana.

Does he have big ears?
Let's just say he's very good at swatting
flies.

Dickie: I hear the team's prospects are
looking up.
Nicky: Oh good, are you leaving it then?

Bob had just missed a shot at goal, which
meant the other team won. "I could kick
myself," he groaned, as the players came
off the pitch.
"Don't bother," said the captain, "you'd
miss."

Golfer: Have you packed all my golf gear in the car?

Wife: Yes, dear: clubs, map, compass, emergency rations . . .

Boy: Have you got any custard left?

Canteen lady: Yes.

Boy: Well you shouldn't have made so much then.

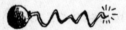

Customer: Two soggy eggs on burnt toast, please.

Café owner: We can't serve that here, sir.

Customer: Why not, you did yesterday.

What happened when the umpire had a brain transplant?
The brain rejected him.

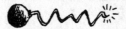

What did they call the crazy golfer?
A crack putt!

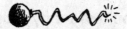

Canteen lady: Do you want more of this custard?
Boy: No thanks, I'm too young to die.

Despondent golfer: I'd move heaven and earth to get a better score.
Caddie: Concentrate on heaven, you've already moved enough earth!

Gloria: Boys fall in love with me at first sight.
Gordon: Yes, but when they take a second look they change their mind!

Harold: We should all try to fight air pollution.
Henry: You could start by stopping breathing.

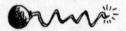

Comedian: Do you find me entertaining?
Friend: I'd say you were too dumb to entertain a thought.

Boss: It would take ten men to fill my shoes.
Secretary, aside: It looks as if it took ten cows to make them.

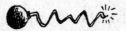

Samantha: Don't I look gorgeous today?
Susannah: It's a treat for people to see you. After all, they have to pay to get into a freak show.

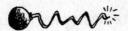

His clothes never go out of style – they look just as old-fashioned every year.

He's so stupid he probably couldn't spell "Anna" backwards.

He can't see further than the nose on his face.
No, but with his nose that's quite a distance.

Diner: Will the band play requests?
Waiter: Yes, sir. What would you like?
Diner: I'd like them to play cards.

I'm as pretty as a flower.
Yes, a cauliflower.

He asked me to tell him everything I know.
I bet you were speechless.

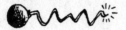

Words fail me.
I'd noticed you don't know how to use
them.

He thinks he's a big cheese.
I certainly have to hold my nose when I'm
near him.

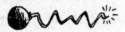

He's such a whinger – if opportunity
knocked he'd complain about the noise.

He's the kind of boy girls dream about.
That's better than seeing him in broad
daylight.

You know how nurses slap babies when
they are born?
Yes.
Well, when you were born I reckon they
took one look and slapped your mother.

What do you think of Ada's looks?
I don't mind her looking, it's her face I
can't stand.

Monty: Does a mud pack help her complexion?
Bunty: It does for a few days, but then the mud falls off.

They say when the photographer took Jim's photograph he never developed it. Why?
He was afraid of being alone with it in a dark room.

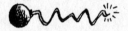

The problem is, his facial features don't seem to understand the importance of being part of a team.

Do you think I have a good complexion?
Let's just say your face is almost as
smooth as a walnut.

Rosie: I like being tickled under the chin.
Josie: Which one?

Nigel has a Roman nose.
Yes, it's roamin' here, roamin
there . . .

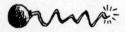

I think she's quite old, don't you?
She has so many wrinkles on her forehead
she has to screw on her hat.

She's not very fat, is she?
No, she's got a really faminine look.
Her sister's skinny, too.
Yes, if she drinks tomato juice she looks
like a thermometer.

Kylie: My uncle's just bought a pig.
Riley: But where will he keep it?
Kylie: Under the bed.
Riley: But what about the smell?
Kylie: The pig will just have to get used to
it.

His death won't be listed under
"Obituaries," it will be under
"Neighborhood Improvements."

She's so ugly that even spiders run away
when they see her.

Susie: I think a lot of people would go to
our principal's funeral.
Sally: Yes, to make sure she's dead!

Kate: I always speak my mind.
Kath: I'm surprised you've so much to say,
then.

Jimmy: Go and squirt lemon juice in your eyes.
Timmy: Whatever for?
Jimmy: It's the only way to make you smart.

You remind me of a toenail.
What do you mean?
The sooner you're cut down to size the better.

What's the difference between a bully and gravy?
Gravy's only thick some of the time.

Stella: You only have one use in life.
Ella: What's that?
Stella: Your face can cure hiccups!

Claud: What's the difference between you and a skunk?
Maud: I don't know.
Claud: You use a cheaper deodorant.

Darren: I'm so thirsty my tongue's hanging out.
Sharon: Is that your tongue? I thought it was a horrible spotted tie!

Bernie: What's the matter with your finger?
Ernie: I think I've got a splinter in it.
Bernie: Have you been scratching your head?

Angus: Have you been talking to yourself again?
Adam: Yes, how did you know?
Angus: You've got that bored look on your face.

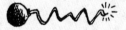

Glyn: You remind me of a builder's bottom.
Wyn: What do you mean?
Glyn: You're full of barefaced cheek!

Patty: What smells worse than a bad egg?
Mattie: I don't know.
Patty: You do!

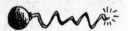

What do you mean she eats like a bird?
She's enormous!
I expect she eats worms.

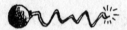

Gilly: Do you like my cottage pie?
Billy: No, it tastes as if you've left the drains in it.

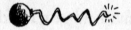

Diner: This food isn't fit for a pig!
Waiter: I'll bring you some that is, sir.

I never forget a face – but in your case I'll make an exception.

Mr Black: I took my wife to the beauty parlor yesterday and I had to sit and wait all afternoon for her.
Mr White: Whatever was she having done?
Mr Black: Nothing – she just went for an estimate.

Mrs Brown: I took my son to the zoo yesterday.
Mrs Green: Did they accept him?

Hear about the stupid builder? He put a notice saying "Stop" on the top of his ladder.

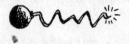

Louise: What's the difference between you and a baby lamb?
Lionel: I don't know.
Louise: The lamb will one day be a sheep, but you'll always be a creep.

Andy: My dad's stronger than your dad.
Mandy: He must be after raising a dumb-bell like you!

Lesley: Did she really call you a creep?
Wesley: Yes. She said I was lower than the fluff in an earthworm's belly button, and if I was any more stupid, I'd have to be watered twice a week.

Cool
Connections

Darren, who was rather fond of Sharon, gave her a box of chocolates at break time on her birthday. "Here you are," he said, blushing, "sweets to the sweet."

"Oh, thanks," said Sharon. "Have a nut."

Hear about the woman who wanted to marry a ghost?
I can't think what possessed her.

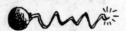

Why did Frankenstein's monster squeeze his girlfriend to death?
He had a crush on her.

1st witch: I'm so unlucky.
2nd witch: Why?
1st witch: Last night I went to a party and met a handsome prince.
2nd witch: What's unlucky about that?
1st witch: When I kissed him he turned into a frog.

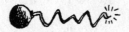

First boy: She had a beautiful pair of eyes, her skin had the glow of a peach, her cheeks were like apples and her lips like cherries – that's my girl.
Second boy: Sounds like a fruit salad to me.

Two men were having a drink together. One said, "I'd rather live with a vampire than with my wife."

"Why's that?" asked the other.

He said, "Because she's always trying to bite my head off."

A lady put a lonely hearts ad in the paper and had a reply which said, "I would love to meet you but I have to tell you that I am eight feet tall, covered in matted fur, with large fangs and slobbering lips. If you still want to meet me then I'll be under the clock in the market square at six o'clock next Saturday."

The lady replied, "I would be interested in meeting you but please will you wear a red carnation and carry a rolled-up newspaper so I can recognize you?"

I bet I could get you to forget about that horrible witch.

What horrible witch?

See, you've forgotten already.

The man tried to poison his wife again.
This time she lay on the floor shouting "Wretch, wretch, wretch!"
He said, "No, you retch – you took the poison."

Who is a vampire likely to fall in love with?
The girl necks door.

Me and the Wife – by Ian Shee.

Who was that I saw you with last night?
It was a girl from the school?
Teacher?
Didn't have to!

When Wally Witherspoon proposed to his girlfriend she said, "I love the simple things in life, Wally, but I don't want one of them for a husband."

A woman was in court charged with wounding her husband. "But madam, why did you stab him over 100 times?" asked the judge.
"Oh, your Honor," replied the defendant, "I didn't know how to switch off the electric carving knife."

Two girls were talking in the corridor.
"That boy over there is getting on my nerves," said Clarrie.
"But he's not even looking at you," replied Clara.
"That's what's getting on my nerves," retorted Clarrie.

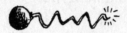

What did the two acrobats say when they got married?
We're head over heels in love!

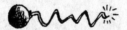

My girlfriend thinks I'm a great wit.
Well, she's half right.

A horrible old witch surprised all her friends by announcing that she was going to get married.

"But," said another old hag, "you always said men were stupid. And you vowed never to marry."

"Yes, I know," said the witch. "But I finally found one who asked me."

"The girl beside me in math is very clever," said Alec to his mother. "She's got enough brain for two."
"Perhaps you'd better think of marriage," said Mom.

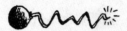

I can't understand why people say my girlfriend's legs look like matchsticks. They do look like sticks – but they certainly don't match.

Ben's new girlfriend uses such greasy lipstick that he has to sprinkle his face with sand to get a better grip.

"What's your new perfume called?" a young man asked his girlfriend.

"High Heaven," she replied.

"I asked what it was called, not what it smells to!"

"What do you do?" a young man asked the beautiful girl he was dancing with.

"I'm a nurse."

"I wish I could be ill and let you nurse me," he whispered in her ear.

"That would be miraculous. I work on the maternity ward."

I'm suffering from bad breath.

You should do something about it! I did. I just sent my wife to the dentist.

"What's the matter?" one man asked another.

"My wife left me when I was in the bath last night," sobbed the second man.

"She must have been waiting for years for the chance," replied the first.

Poor old Stephen sent his photograph off to a Lonely Hearts Club.

They sent it back saying that they weren't that lonely.

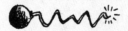

Freddie had persuaded Amanda to marry him, and was formally asking her father for his permission. "Sir," he said, "I would like to have your daughter for my wife."

"Why can't she get one of her own?" replied Amanda's father.

Why aren't you married?
I was born that way.

Mrs Jones and her little daughter Karen were outside the church watching all the comings and goings of a wedding. After the photographs had been taken, everyone had driven off to the reception and all the excitement was over, Karen said to her mother, "Why did the bride change her mind, Mommy?"
"How do you mean, change her mind?" asked Mrs Jones.
"Well," said the moppet, "she went into the church with one man and came out with another."

Why did you refuse to marry Richard, Tessa?
'Cos he said he would die if I didn't and I'm just curious.

My Peter keeps telling everyone he's going to marry the most beautiful girl in the world.
What a shame! And after all the time you've been engaged!

"But she's so young to get married," sobbed Diana's mother. "Only seventeen!"
"Try not to cry about it," said her husband soothingly. "Think of it not as losing a daughter but as gaining a bathroom."

"Doctor Sawbones speaking."
"Oh, doctor, my wife's just dislocated her jaw. Can you come over in, say, three or four weeks' time?"

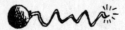

A salesman was trying to persuade a housewife to buy a life insurance policy. "Just imagine, if your husband were to die," he said. "What would you get?"
"Oh, a sheepdog, I think," replied the wife. "They're so well-behaved."

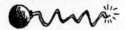

My wife says that if I don't give up golf she'll leave me.
Say, that's tough, old man.
Yeah, I'm going to miss her.

Mrs Brown was always complaining about her husband. "If things go on like this I'll have to leave him," she moaned to Mrs Jenkins.

"Give him the soft-soap treatment," said Mrs Jenkins.

"I tried that," replied Mrs Brown, "it didn't work. He spotted it at the top of the stairs."

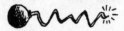

Mommy, mommy, why do you keep poking daddy in the ribs? If I don't, the fire will go out.

Mr Brown: I hate to tell you, but your wife just fell in the wishing well.
Mr Smith: It works!

My husband really embarrassed me yesterday. We were at the vicarage for tea and he drank his with his little finger sticking out.

But that's considered polite in some circles.

Not with the teabag hanging from it, it's not.

Wife to husband: I'll have you know I've got the face of a teenager!

Husband to wife: Then you should give it back, you're wearing it out.

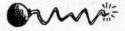

Bill: What would it take to make you give me a kiss?

Gill: An anesthetic.

Harry: I've a soft spot for you.

Mary: Really?

Harry: Yes, in the middle of a bog!

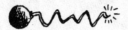

James: I call my girlfriend Peach.

John: Because she's beautiful?

James: No, because she's got a heart of stone!

Romeo: I'd go to the end of the earth for you.

Juliet: Good. And when you get there, jump off!

My boyfriend only has two faults –
everything he says and everything he does!

They say he has a leaning towards blondes.
Yes, but they keep pushing him back.

Judge: Your first three wives died from eating poisonous mushrooms, and now your fourth wife has drowned in your swimming-pool. Isn't that all a bit odd?

Prisoner: Not really. She didn't like mushrooms.

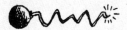

I hear she doesn't care for a man's company.

Not unless he owns it.

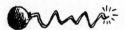

My sister fell in love at second sight. When she first met him she didn't know how rich he was.

I got a gold watch for my girlfriend.
I wish I could make a trade like that!

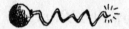

What do you call pigs who live together?
Pen pals.

What's the best way to get rid of excess fat?
Divorce him.

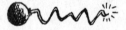

When my mom and dad got engaged she asked him if he would be giving her a ring. He said, "Of course. What's your number?"

What will you do when you're as big as your dad?
Go on a diet!

Eskimo girl: There's something I'd like to give you.
Eskimo boy: What?
Eskimo girl: The cold shoulder.

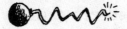

Wife: Did you like the food I cooked for you?
Husband: Let's just say it was a real swill dinner.

Barney: My girlfriend's cooking's like a good man.
Arnie: What do you mean?
Barney: Hard to keep down!

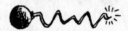

Wife: Did you really marry me because you'd heard my uncle had left me a fortune?
Husband: No, I'd have married you no matter who had left you a fortune.

My wife is very dear to me.
Yes, I believe she costs you a fortune.

My husband's a millionaire.
He was a multi-millionaire before you married him.

My girlfriend loves nature.
That's very good of her, considering what nature has done for her!

How are you getting on with James?
Well, he's a bit dull until you get to know him.
And when you have got to know him you'll find he's a real bore!

He is pretty boring.
Yes, but he does have occasional moments
of silence.

Husband: You took me for better or worse.
Wife: Yes, but I didn't think it would be
this much worse.

Saul: My wife worships me.
Paul: Why do you think that?
Saul: She puts burnt offerings in front of
me three times a day.

Wife: One more word from you and I'm going back to Mother!
Husband: Taxi!

They say he's her idol.
He certainly never does anything.

Myron: I can marry anyone I please!
Byron: But you don't please anyone!

Wife: We've been married 12 whole months.
Husband: Seems more like a year to me.

Wife: I've given you the best years of my life.
Husband: Are you asking me for a receipt?

Foreign visitor: And is this your most charming wife?
Husband: No, she's the only one I've got.

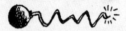

She talks so much he's never on speaking terms with her, just listening terms!

What do you call two elephants who leave their wedding on a bicycle?
Optimistic.

Can your husband cook?
Let's just say that yesterday he burned
the salad.

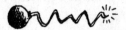

Why do you call your girlfriend Treasure?
Because I wonder where she was dug up!

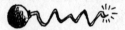

Kerry: My girlfriend's different from all
other girls.
Terry: I bet she's different. She's the
only girl around who'll go out with you!

How did Ann find out she'd married an
elephant?
By the "E" on his pajamas.

When he told me he loved me he said he'd go through anything for me.
And has he?
So far he's only gone through my bank account.

Billy: Since I met you I haven't been able to eat or drink.
Tilly: Because you love me so much?
Billy: No, because I'm broke.

Young man: I've come to ask for your daughter's hand.
Father: You'll have to take the rest of her too or the deal's off.

Why do they call her an after-dinner speaker?
Because every time she speaks to a man she's after a dinner.

William: Bob's so suspicious, isn't he?
Wilfred: Yes. Even his eyes watch each other all the time.

Stan: You remind me of the sea.
Sue: Because I'm so wild and romantic?
Stan: No, because you make me sick!

Tom: Could you be happy with a boy like me?
Trish: Maybe, if you weren't around too often.

Jack: I was chosen by a computer as being an ideal boyfriend.
John: A computer's about the only thing that would have you as a boyfriend.

If we get married do you think you'll be able to live on my income?
Of course. But what will you live on?

Mrs Rose: Where are you going to?
Mrs Thorn: The doctor's. I don't like the look of my husband.
Mrs Rose: Can I come with you? I can't stand the sight of mine!

Holly: How are you getting on with your advertisements for a husband? Have you had any replies?

Molly: Yes, lots. And they all say the same – take mine!

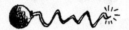

Clark: I'm not rich like Arwin, and I don't have a country estate like Brian or a Ferrari like Clive, but I love you and I want to marry you.

Clara: I love you too, but what did you say about Brian?

Husband: Let's go out tonight and have some fun.

Wife: Yes let's, but if you get home before I do, leave the light on please.

Brian: Why are you covered with scratches?

Byron: My girlfriend said it with flowers.

Brian: That sounds romantic.

Byron: It wasn't, she hit me round the head with a bunch of roses.

Samantha: Do you really love me?

Simon: Oh yes.

Samantha: Then whisper something soft and sweet in my ear.

Simon: Lemon meringue pie.

Wife: Today we're having Chicken Surprise.

Husband: What's the surprise?

Wife: You're cooking it.

Bridegroom: Will you really be able to put up with me for the rest of your life?
Bride: Of course, dear, you'll be out at work most of the time!

First man: Is your wife fat?
Second man: Put it this way, when we were married and I carried her across the threshold I had to make two trips.

Romeo: Will you come to the movies with me tonight?
Juliet: Oh no, I never go out with perfect strangers.
Romeo: Who says I'm perfect?

Juliet: Whisper those three little words
that will make my day.
Romeo: Go to hell!

They say she's been asked to get married
hundreds of times.
Really? Who by?
Her parents!

Ice
Breakers

Why did the cat put the letter "M" into the fridge?
Because it turns ice into mice.

Why is a polar bear cheap to have as a pet?
It lives on ice.

What was the fly doing on the ice cream?
Learning to ski.

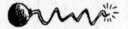

What kind of money do yetis use?
Iced lolly.

What does a yeti eat for dinner?
Iceburgers.

How do ghosts like their drinks?
Ice ghoul.

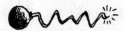

What do you get if you cross a witch with an iceberg?
A cold spell.

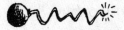

Two witches lost their brooms and crash-landed on an iceberg.
"Do you think we'll be here long?" asked the first.
"No," said the second, "here comes the Titanic."

Waiter, waiter! What's this cockroach doing on my ice-cream sundae?
I think it's skiing downhill.

What happened when the ice monster had a furious row with the zombie?
He gave him the cold shoulder.

What's the difference between an iced lolly and the school bully?
You lick one, the others lick you.

What happened when the ice monster ate a curry?
He blew his cool.

Simon: My girlfriend and I fell out last night. She wanted to go and watch ice-skating, but I wanted to go to the football match.
Peter: What was the ice-skating like?

What takes a lot of licks from a teacher without complaint?
An ice cream.

Wally: If frozen water is iced water, what is frozen ink?
Sally: Iced ink.

On their first evening in their new home the bride went into the kitchen to fix the drinks.

Five minutes she came back into the living-room in tears.

"What's the matter, my angel?" asked her husband anxiously.

"Oh Derek!" she sobbed, "I put the ice-cubes in hot water to wash them and they've disappeared!"

What did Tom get when he locked Jerry in the freezer?
Mice cubes.

Why did Ken keep his trumpet in the fridge?
Because he liked cool music.

A family of tortoises went into a café for some ice cream. They sat down and were about to start when Father Tortoise said, "I think its gong to rain, Junior, will you pop home and fetch my umbrella?"

So off went Junior for Father's umbrella, but three days later he still hadn't returned. "I think, dear," said Mother Tortoise to Father Tortoise, "that we had better eat Junior's ice cream before it melts."

And a voice from the door said, "If you do that I won't go."

Teacher: Order, children, order!
Daft Derek: Two chocolate ice creams and three orange lollipops, please.

What did the Eskimo schoolboy say to the Eskimo schoolgirl?
What's an ice girl like you doing in a place like this?

One very hot day an extremely small man went into a café, put his newspaper on a table and went to the counter. But on returning with a cup of tea he saw that his place had been taken by a huge, bearded, ferocious-looking man of some 300 pounds in weight, and six feet nine inches in height. "Excuse me," said the little man to the big man, "but you're sitting in my seat." "Oh yeah?" snarled the big man. "Prove it!" "Certainly. You're sitting on my ice cream."

Notice by a village pond: Beware! All of this ice is frozen.

Why did Darren put his father in the freezer?
He wanted ice-cold pop.

How do you know if an elephant's been in your fridge?
There are footprints in the butter.

Why did the stupid witch keep her clothes in the fridge?
She liked to have something cool to slip into in the evening.

A woman went to the fridge to get some milk and all she found was a disembodied hand there.
It was all fingers and thumbs.

Cannibal Boy: I've brought a friend home for dinner.
Cannibal Mom: Put him in the fridge and we'll have him tomorrow.

What do you call the famous Italian artist who did his paintings sitting on the fridge?
Bottichilli.

Did you hear about the mad scientist who put dynamite in his fridge?
They say he blew his cool.

What stays hot in the fridge?
A hamburger with too much mustard on it.

What did the mayonnaise say to the fridge?
"Shut the door, I'm dressing."

What is brown one minute and white the next?
A rat in a deep-freeze.

Angela had to write down on her exam paper the name of a liquid that won't freeze, so she wrote "hot water."

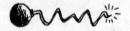

What did the Eskimo children sing when one of their class was leaving school?
"Freeze a Jolly Good Fellow."

Why did the monster drink ten liters of anti-freeze?
So that he didn't have to buy a winter coat.

Why did the snowman call his dog Frost?
Because frost bites.

What's another way to describe a duck?
A chicken with snowshoes.

What exams do yetis take?
Snow levels.

Can the Abominable Snowman jump very high?
Hardly – he can only just clear his throat!

Teacher: Who knows what we mean by the Cold War?
Larry: Err, a snowball fight?

What kind of man doesn't like to sit in front of the fire?
An Abominable Snowman.

How do Abominable Snowmen feel when they melt?
Abominable!

What do Abominable Snowmen call their offspring?
Chill-dren.

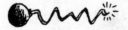

Where do Abominable Snowmen go to dance?
To snowballs.

What did one Abominable Snowman say to the other?
I'm afraid I just don't believe in people.

What is the Abominable Snowman's favorite book?
War and Frozen Peas.

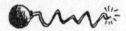

What did the Abominable Snowman do after he had had his teeth pulled out?
He ate the dentist.

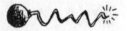

Why did the skeleton stay out in the snow all night?
He was a numbskull.

I Met An Abominable Snowman – by Anne
Tarctic.

There was a young yeti from Gloucester
Whose granny and grandfather lost 'er.
Next day she was found
In the snow-covered ground
But they didn't know how to defrost her.

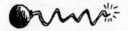

Doctor, doctor! I keep thinking I'm the
Abominable Snowman.
Keep cool.

What does it mean if you have an elephant in your fridge?
He slept over, after the great party you had last night.

Did you hear about the woman who was so keen on road safety that she always wore white at night?
Last winter she was knocked down by a snow plow.

Billy: I never had a sled when I was a kid. We were too poor.
Milly, feeling sorry for him: What a shame! What did you do when it snowed?
Billy: Slid down the hills on my cousin.

Why was the snowman no good at playing in the big match?
He got cold feet.

Ted and Fred were enjoying themselves in the snow. "You can borrow my sled if you like," said Ted.
"Thanks," said Fred. "We'll share it, shall we?"
"Yes," said Ted. "I'll have it going downhill and you can have it going uphill."

Cooler
Cracks

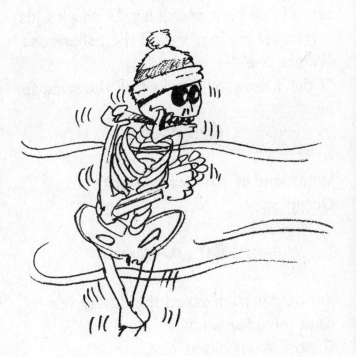

Two shark fishermen were sitting on the side of their boat just off the coast of Florida, cooling their feet in the sea. Suddenly an enormous shark swam up and bit off one fisherman's leg. "A shark's just bitten off my leg," yelled the fisherman. "Which one?"
"I don't know, all sharks look the same to me."

What kind of cats love water?
Octopusses.

Bertie: My mom asked the doctor for something for wind.
Gertie: What did he do?
Bertie: He gave her a kite.

Kevin: I'm really cool, you know.
Kieran: I always thought you were a cold fish.

Why is a football stadium cool?
It's full of fans.

How do you know if your cat's got a bad cold?
He has cat-arrh.

What do you give a pony with a cold?
Cough stirrup.

What does an octopus wear when it's cold?
A coat of arms.

What goes "hum-choo, hum-choo"?
A bee with a cold.

What's a cold, evil candle called?
The wicked wick of the north.

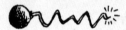

What kind of medicine does Dracula take
for a cold?
Coffin medicine.

What happened to the zombie who had a bad cold?
He said, "I'm dead-up wid fuddy jokes aboud zondies."

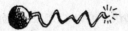

Werewolf: Doctor, doctor, thank you so much for curing me.
Doctor: So you don't think you're a werewolf anymore?
Werewolf: Absolutely not, I'm quite clear now – see my nose is nice and cold.

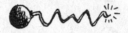

Doctor, doctor! What would you take for this cold?
Make me an offer.

Why do skeletons hate winter?
Because the cold goes right through them.

Doctor, doctor! How can I stop my cold
going to my chest?
Tie a knot in your neck.

Doctor, doctor! I keep thinking I'm a dog
out in the cold.
Oh, stop whining.

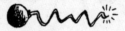

What happened when the ice monster had
a furious row with the zombie?
He gave him the cold shoulder.

And what goes into the water pink and comes out blue?
A swimmer on a cold day!

What's hairy and damp and sits shivering at fairs?
A coconut with a cold.

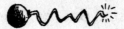

What's the difference between a bus driver and a cold?
One knows the stops; the other stops the nose.

What is hairy and coughs?
A coconut with a cold.

George knocked on the door of his friend's house.
When his friend's mother answered he said: "Can Albert come out to play?"
"No," said the mother, "it's too cold."
"Well, then," said George. "can his football come out to play?"

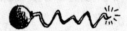

Geography teacher: What is the coldest place in the world?
Ann: Chile.

What can a schoolboy keep and give away
at the same time?
A cold.

Did you hear about the snake with a bad
cold?
No! Tell me about the snake with a bad
cold.
She had to viper nose.

Why can you run faster when you've got a
cold?
Because you have a racing pulse and a
running nose.

Teacher: Matthew, what is the climate of New Zealand?

Matthew: Very cold, sir.

Teacher: Wrong.

Matthew: But sir! When they send us meat, it always arrives frozen!

Lady (to a tramp who's asked for a meal): Do you like cold prunes and custard?

Tramp: I love it, lady.

Lady: Well, call back later, it is very hot right now.

Young Horace was being taught how to box, but so far hadn't landed a single blow on his opponent.

"Don't worry, lad," said his teacher, "keep swinging – the draft might give him a cold."

It was raining, and the goalie had let several goals through. As he came off the pitch he sniffed, and said, "I think I've caught a cold."

"I'm pleased to hear you can catch something," replied a fellow player.

It was a warm day and the baseball player kept missing his shots. After the match he sighed and said, "What couldn't I do with a long, cold drink?"

"Hit it?" inquired a fellow player.

Billy: Is your cold better?
Tilly: I've got a very bad head but I hope to shake it off soon.

He's so cold-blooded that if a mosquito bit him it would get pneumonia.

You're like a summer cold!
What do you mean?
It's impossible to get rid of you!

What animal with two humps can be found at the North Pole?
A lost camel.

Neddy: I've got a cold in the head.
Teddy: It must be the first time you've had anything in your head.

How do sheep keep warm in winter?
Central bleating.

What likes to spend the summer in a fur coat and the winter in a swimsuit?
A moth.

First cat: Where do fleas go in winter?
Second cat: Search me!

Waiter, waiter! There's a wasp in my pudding.
So that's where they go to in the winter.

Why don't vultures fly south in the winter?
Because they can't afford the air fare.

Why did the canoeist take a water pistol
with him?
So he could shoot the rapids.

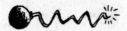

What's thick, black, floats on water and
shouts "Knickers!"?
Crude oil.

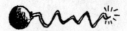

What do you get if you cross a bottle of
water with an electric eel?
A bit of a shock really!

What insect can fly underwater?
A bluebottle in a submarine

Teacher: Why do birds fly south in winter?
Jim: Because it's too far to walk.

What happens if you upset a cannibal?
You get into hot water.

What do you call a witch who likes the beach but is scared of the water?
A chicken sand-witch.

Why are vampire families so close?
Because blood is thicker than water.

What do you call an alien starship that drips water?
A crying saucer.

"Now don't forget boys," the science teacher droned on, "If it wasn't for water we would never learn to swim. And if we'd never learned to swim, just think how many people would have drowned!"

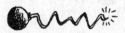

That boy is so dirty, the only time he washes his ears is when he eats watermelon.

Did you hear about the idiot who made his chickens drink boiling water?
He thought they would lay hard-boiled eggs.

Teacher: Martin, put some more water in the fish tank.
Martin: But, Sir, they haven't drunk the water I gave them yesterday.

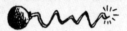

Mrs Twigg took her class on a nature ramble. They went past a large duck pond. "Be careful not to fall in, children," she said, "the water's very deep."
"But it can't be, Miss," said Susie, "it only comes up to the middle of those ducks."

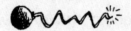

Why did the music student have a piano in the bathroom?
Because he was practicing Handel's Water Music.

Doctor, doctor! I think I've been bitten by a vampire.

Drink this glass of water.

Will it make me better?

No, but I'll be able to see if your neck leaks.

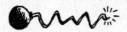

Anne: Ugh! The water in my glass is cloudy.

Dan, trying to impress his new girlfriend: It's all right, it's just the glass that hasn't been washed.

Daddy, daddy, can I have another glass of water please?

But that's the tenth one I've given you tonight.

Yes, but the baby's bedroom is still on fire.

When is the water in the shower room musical?
When it's piping hot.

Why did the teacher wear a lifejacket at night?
Because she liked sleeping on a waterbed, and couldn't swim!

Which is the ghost's favorite stretch of water?
Lake Eerie.

Cooler Cracks

Did you hear about the stupid water-polo player?
His horse drowned . . .

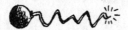

The food at the club dinner was awful. The soup tasted like dishwater, the fish was off, the meat was overcooked, and the vegetables were obviously old. The last straw for one member was the custard, which was thick and lumpy. "This meal is disgusting!" he roared. "And what's more, I'm going to bring it up at the annual board meeting next week!"

What is full of holes but can hold water?
A sponge.

A man in a swimming pool was on the very top diving board. He poised, lifted his arms, and was about to dive when the attendant came running up, shouting, "Don't dive – there's no water in that pool!"
"That's all right," said the man. "I can't swim!"

Policeman: Why are you driving with a bucket of water on the passenger seat?
Motorist: So I can dip my headlights.

Jane: Have you noticed that your mother smells a bit funny these days?
Wayne: No. Why?
Jane: Well, your sister told me she was giving her a bottle of toilet water for her birthday.

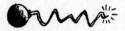

Sign in a café: The management has personally passed all drinking water in this establishment.

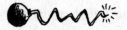

He's so dumb that after he'd watched a gardening program on TV he started watering the light bulbs.

I hear he's a very careful person.
Well, he likes to economize on soap and water.

What happened to the yacht that sank in shark-infested waters?
It came back with a skeleton crew.

Why didn't the idiot go water-skiing when he was on holiday?
He couldn't find a sloping lake.

Notice by a river: When this sign is under water the towpath is flooded.

Mrs Green: How's your new house?

Mrs Brown: The roof needs mending. In last week's storm, rain was coming down the walls like water.

Bob: They say he has a waterproof voice.

Ted: What do you mean?

Bob: It can't be drowned out.

If we want to keep our heads above water
we must keep our ears to the ground.

Ronnie: Why are you bathing in such dirty
water?
Donnie: It wasn't dirty when I got in it.

How can I cure water on the knee?
Wear pumps.

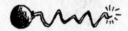

Why do watermelons have to have a formal
wedding?
Because they cant-elope.

Did you hear about the sailor that was discharged from the submarine service? He was caught sleeping with the windows open.

Wasps – while everyone runs a mile when they see one, why does it take hours for them to work out how to get out of a room, even after you've opened the window that they're standing on?

Doctor: You need new glasses.
Monster: How did you guess?
Doctor: I could tell the moment you walked through the window.

Doctor, doctor! I keep thinking I'm a moth.
So why did you come to see me?
Well, I saw the light in the window . . .

A wizard went to the doctor one day
complaining of headaches. "It's because I
live in the same room as two of my
brothers," he said. "One of them has six
goats and the other has four pigs and they
all live in the room with us. The smell is
terrible."
"Well couldn't you just open the windows?"
asked the doctor.
"Certainly not," he replied, "my bats would
fly out."

Art teacher: What color would you paint the sun and the wind?
Brian: The sun rose, and the wind blue.

How did the teacher forecast the weather with a piece of string?
She hung it up, and if it moved, she knew it was windy, and if it got wet, she knew it was raining.

Why does the Hound of the Baskervilles turn round and round before he lies down for the night?
Because he's the watchdog and he has to wind himself up.

Doctor, doctor! I think I'm Napoleon.
How long have you felt like this?
Since Waterloo.

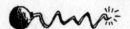

Mr Jones met a neighbor carrying a front
door. "Why are you carrying that, Tom?"
asked Mr Jones.
"I've lost my key," replied Tom.
"Oh," said Mr Jones, "so how will you get
in?"
"It's all right – I've left the window open."

Who broke the window?
It was Andrew, Dad. He ducked when I
threw a stone at him.

A jeweler standing behind the counter of his shop was astounded to see a man come hurtling head first through the window. "What on earth are you up to?" he demanded.

"I'm terribly sorry," said the man, "I forgot to let go of the brick!"

How do you cure a headache?
Put your head through a window, and the pane will disappear.

Sign in shop window: FOR SALE Pedigree bulldog. Housebroken. Eats anything. Very fond of children.

A man is in a prison cell with no windows and no doors; there are no holes in the ceiling or trapdoors in the floor, yet in the morning the wardens find him gone. How did he get out?

Through the doorway – there were no doors remember!

At a very posh wedding, one of the guests broke wind. The bridegroom was furious and rounded on the guilty party. "How dare you break wind in front of my wife?" he roared.

"Sorry," said the guest. "Was it her turn?"

"Gosh, it's raining cats and dogs," said Suzie looking out of the kitchen window.
"I know," said her mother who had just come in. "I've just stepped in a poodle!"

Dad, there's a man at the door collecting for the new swimming pool.
Give him a glass of water!

Who was the first underwater spy?
James Pond.

What happened when the bell fell in the water?
It got wringing wet.

Don't look out of the window, Lavinia, people will think it's Hallowe'en.

Dylan: I take lots of exercise.
Duncan: I thought so. That's why you're so long-winded.

What happened to the man who couldn't tell putty from custard?
His windows fell out.

What happened to the man who couldn't tell the difference between putty and porridge?
His teeth stuck together and his windows fell out.

Father: George! Don't let the dog hang his head out of the window whilst driving!

Red Hot
Funnies

What do you get if you pour hot water down a rabbit hole?
Hot cross bunnies!

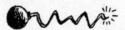

It was so hot when we went on holiday last year that we had to take turns sitting in each other's shadow.

What do you get if you cross a snake with a hot dog?
A fangfurter.

What do frogs drink?
Hot croako.

What's white on the outside, green on the inside and comes with relish and onions?
A hot frog.

What happens if you eat a hot frog?
You croak in no time.

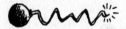

What is the proper name for the water otter?
A kettle.

What do witches ring for in a hotel?
B-room service.

1st cannibal: I don't know what to make of my husband.
2nd cannibal: How about a hotpot?

Hey, Waiter, you've got your thumb in my bowl of soup!
Don't worry, sir, the soup isn't hot.

It was sweltering hot outside. The teacher came into the classroom wiping his brow and said, "Ninety-two today. Ninety-two."
"Happy birthday to you. Happy birthday to you . . ." sang the class.

When the class went on a trip to the seaside, they stayed at a small hotel that advertised Bed and Board. The trouble was, they said afterwards, it was difficult to know which was the bed and which was the board.

What did the teacher say after spending thousands in the expensive hotel?
"I'm sorry to leave, now that I've almost bought the place."

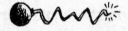

Tarzan, coming home after a hard day's work: "Jane, it's a jungle out there."

A man arrived at a seaside hotel where he had made a reservation rather late at night. All the lights were out, so he knocked on the door. After a long time a light appeared in an upstairs window and a woman called out, "Who are you? What do you want?"

"I'm staying here."

"Stay there, then," she retorted, and slammed the window shut!

Teacher: I'd like a room, please.
Hotel receptionist: Single, Sir?
Teacher: Yes, but I am engaged.

There was a little old lady from a small town in America who had to go to Texas. She was amazed at the size of her hotel and her suite. She went into the huge café and said to the waitress, who took her order for a cup of coffee, that she had never before seen anything as big as the hotel or her suite. "Everything's big in Texas, ma'am," said the waitress. The coffee came in the biggest cup the old lady had ever seen. "I told you, ma'am that everything is big in Texas," said the waitress. On her way back to her suite, the old lady got lost in the vast corridors. She opened the door of a darkened room and fell into an enormous swimming pool. "Please!" she screamed. "Don't flush it!"

When we got to Benidorm the hotel was so full I had to sleep on a door across two tables. Was it comfortable?
Oh yes, but a bit drafty around the letter-box.

"Is my dinner hot?" asked the excessively late husband. "It should be," said his furious wife, "it's been on the fire since seven o'clock!"

Did you hear about the ghoul's favorite hotel?
It had running rot and mould in every room.

I was a waiter at the Hotel Splendiferous for three months, but I had to leave on account of the head waiter's nerves.
His nerves?
He couldn't stand the sound of breaking crockery.

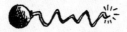

John: Do you feel like a cup of tea?
Don: Oh, yes.
John: You look like one, too – sloppy, hot and wet!

There were two eggs boiling in a saucepan.
One said "Phew, it's hot in here."
The other said, "Wait till you get out, you'll get your head bashed in."

Hotel porter: May I carry your bag, sir?
Hotel guest: That won't be necessary, my wife is perfectly capable of walking.

What's green and served hot from the oven?
An idiot's salad.

How do you stop someone who's been working out in the gym on a hot day from smelling?
Put a peg on his nose!

What's the hottest letter of the alphabet?
"B." It makes oil boil.

Did you hear about the two men who were cremated at the same time?
It was a dead heat.

What's the difference between Father
Christmas and a warm dog?
Father Christmas wears a whole suit, a dog
just pants.

What do you get if you cross an elephant
with some locusts?
I'm not sure, but if they ever swarm –
watch out!

How do mice celebrate when they move
house?
With a mouse-warming party.

What did the drone say to the Queen Bee?
"Swarm in here isn't it?"

Why does a witch wear a pointed black hat?
To keep her head warm.

Teacher: What do you think astronauts wear to keep warm?
Girl: Apollo neck jumpers?

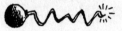

Bill: This loaf is nice and warm!
Tim: It should be – the cat's been sitting on it all day!

Eddie was telling Freddie of his plans to make a lot of money.

"I intend to buy a dozen swarms of bees and every morning at dawn I'm going to let them into the park opposite my house to spend all the day making honey, while I relax."

"But the park doesn't open until nine o'clock," protested Freddie.

"I realize that," said Eddie, "but I know where there's a hole in the fence."

Darren was showing Sharon his holiday photos. She admired all the scenery and the people. Then Darren showed her a picture of him having a donkey ride on the beach. "Who's that on your back?" asked Sharon.

What was proved when the fat man was run over by a steamroller?
That he had a lot of guts.

Why did the farmer plow his field with a steamroller?
Because he planned to grow mashed potatoes.

"Your son is horribly spoiled," a woman said to a proud mother one day.
"How dare you!" retorted the second woman. "My son's a perfect little gentleman."
"I'm afraid you haven't seen what the steamroller's done to him!"

What's the difference between
Frankenstein and boiled potatoes?
You can't mash Frankenstein.

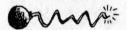

1st cannibal: Come and have dinner in our
hut tonight.
2nd cannibal: What are you having?
1st cannibal: Hard-boiled legs.

What do you call an English teacher, five
feet tall, covered from head to toe in boils
and totally bald?
Sir!

Psychiatrist: Well, what's your problem?

Patient: I prefer brown shoes to black shoes.

Psychiatrist: There's nothing wrong with that. Lots of people prefer brown shoes to black shoes. I do myself.

Patient: Really? How do you like yours – fried or boiled?

Wife, to husband: Boil the baby while I feed the potatoes, will you?

Heather: Help! I'm boiling!

Hyacinth: Oh, simmer down.

Giles: Can you lend me 10 cents? I want to phone a friend.
Miles: Here's 25 cents. Phone all your friends.

Doctor: Nurse, how is that little boy doing – the one who swallowed all those quarters?
Nurse: No change yet.

CONTENTS

THE
CONTRIBUTORS

(1)
Sarah Chan

Sarah, a Hong-Kong born Chinese, came to live and study in Great Britain in 1976. She lives in N.W. London, and has been working for Christian Witness To Israel in London since 1982.

(2)
J. Douglas MacMillan

Shortly after providing his written account, Douglas died suddenly on Saturday 3rd, August 1991. In his contribution to this book, he has left a challenging account of his conversion and subsequent service for Christ first as a pastor in Aberdeen and Glasgow, then as a Professor of Church History before returning to pastor Buccleuch Free Church in Edinburgh. Douglas was highly regarded, and is greatly missed.

'...Blessed are the dead who die in the Lord from now on.'

'Yes,' says the Spirit, 'they will rest from their labour, for their deeds will follow them' (Rev.14:13).

5

(3)
Anne Rayment

Anne is thirty-three and lives in Chester, England. She is married to Charles and has two daughters. She works part-time as a sales agent and has written two novels for teenagers, *A Different Mary* and *Only Children* both published by Christian Focus. Her chief interest is youth work, and she is involved with Barnardo's as well as running a youth group with Charles at Upton Baptist Church.

(4)
Gurnam Singh

Gurnam was born in Nairobi, Kenya and lived there for twenty years before coming to Britain in 1980. He is married to Julia and they have a daughter Esther Rani, who was born in 1990. They live in Glasgow where Gurnam works as a minister with the Free Church of Scotland.

(5)
Jeanette Fyfe

Jeanette grew up in Aberdare in South Wales. Her family belonged to a local Jehovah's Witnesses group. After the failure of their prophecy concerning the end of the world in 1975, she began to search for the true way of knowing God. She now stays in Dingwall, Scotland where she attends a Christian church. She is married to Richard and has two children.

(6)
Malcolm MacLean

Malcolm was born in Inverness, Scotland in 1953, the oldest of three brothers. He and his wife, Katie, live in Inverness where he is an elder in an evangelical church. Since 1989 he has been involved in Christian publishing.

(7)
Elizabeth Rose

Elizabeth Rose was born in 1924 at Kilravock Castle, near Inverness where she still lives. She was in the WRNS from 1944-1946. She has had the responsibility of the estate since she was twenty-one when her father died as her brother was previously killed at El Alamein. She was a secretary in the south of England for some years but on the death of her mother in 1966 prepared for the Castle to be a Christian Guest House which has proved, with the Lord's help, to be very successful and a source of blessing both to the staff and the guests.

(8)
Donald Macleod

Donald is married to Mary, and stays in Edinburgh. He is Professor of Systematic Theology in the Free Church College. He has written several books, including *Behold Your God*, *The Spirit Of Promise* and *Rome And Canterbury, A View From Geneva*.

(9)
Margo Macaskill

Margo was born in 1943 at her family home in Ferintosh on the Black Isle in northern Scotland. She is the seventh youngest in a family of nine. She is now living in Dundee and is married to Donald C. Macaskill who is minister at Dens Road Church. They have two children, a son aged eighteen and a daughter of twelve. She is a housewife and a registered childminder. Some of the children she looks after are handicapped.

(10)
Tony

Tony is married and is the father of two boys. He suffers from multiple sclerosis. Despite being bedbound he is a cheerful witness to his Saviour. 'The more I read the Bible, the more I believe' sums up his attitude to the Word of God, in which he has found tremendous comfort. Because of personal circumstances, his surname has been withheld.

1

He Found Me - Sarah Chan

"You're a daughter of Kun-Yan," my mother said.

Every morning and evening my mother placed two sticks of burning incense into a little tin pot in front of a small oriental-looking wooden doll named Kun-Yan. Then Mother would say to me, "Give Kun-Yan three bows." Kun-Yan wore a radiant long red dress. Her hair was very black and full, tightly tied back in a long tail. There were also colourful ribbons, small bows and pearl pins in her hair. She looked gentle and beautiful. There was a soft smile on her face. I always thought that Kun-Yan was pretty. Once or twice, I was tempted to touch her when Mother was not at home, but somehow I was too frightened to do it. I spoke to Kun-Yan every day. She knew all my secrets. I often asked my mother questions about Kun-Yan. She said that Kun-Yan was with Buddha for a long time and flew to live with us from heaven. It was the earliest memory of my childhood, and the first knowledge I had about gods.

How God led me to Jesus

I was born in Hong Kong, the only child of Chinese parents. When I was six my mother died. I did not really know her very well. Father often told me that Mother was a keen Buddhist. He said that we should respect Mother's wishes and religion, and that I must continue to burn incense and pray to her regularly.

After the death of Mother, Father had been invited by friends to a Christian church and took me with him. I also attended a Christian primary school. I began to hear stories about Jesus, but Jesus was so different from Kun-Yan. Unlike Kun-Yan, Jesus had blue eyes, pale white skin and fair hair. He was not Chinese. I was very fascinated by the pictures and stories of Jesus. I also realized that Mother had lied to me about Kun-Yan that she flew to us from the sky. Kun-Yan was only a man-made little wooden idol.

I, therefore, came to the conclusion that Buddhism was not a true religion. Furthermore, Jesus' stories were so fascinating and interesting to me. I really thought, and gradually believed, that Jesus must be God. I prayed to him regularly, but only when I needed help or wanted something. (Briefly and hastily I prayed every night, "Jesus, please wake me up at seven o'clock in the morning. Amen.")

Being an only child, I was totally spoiled by my father, but sometimes he was strict, particularly about my school work. Although I did quite well in school, Father still paid a private tutor to teach me. He would save every penny for my education. When he was on his own at lunch, he only had a small piece of Tofu (soya bean-curd, which was the cheapest food) and a bowl of plain rice, but he always bought me things which I liked. For instance, I loved mangoes. They were comparatively expensive because they were imported seasonal fruits. I only had them occasionally as a real treat, such as when I received good reports in school. One day, Father bought me five mangoes, and said that I might have one a day. However, I finished them all in one day! The next day, to my great surprise, I found another four, huge, juicy mangoes on the table!

I 'bargained' with Father nearly every Sunday when he wanted me to go to church. He had to either take me out for Dim Sum (Chinese Breakfast in a restaurant), or give me extra pocket money. I did not like to go to church. I found Sunday School very boring. One Sunday, I pleaded with Father and asked him to take me to a Communion service ('Holy Meal' in literal Chinese). I was very curious about that special 'meal' the grown ups had in their service. I was,

of course, extremely disappointed by the experience of my first 'Holy Meal'! It was not a meal, certainly not the feast which I had eagerly anticipated, and I did not understand the service.

One particular bargain, I remember, I was quite satisfied with. It was for a new dress and fifty dollars to spend during my summer vacation. It was not our usual Sunday bargaining. Father wanted me to join the church's Youth Summer Camp. He always thought that the church would be good for me. He liked me to mix with the 'good' people in the church. Although I really did not want to 'waste' a week of my Summer holiday with the 'church people', I felt that Father would be pleased so I agreed to attend the camp. Obviously I could not resist the thought of a new dress and extra pocket money for the vacation. Therefore, I willingly attended the Summer Youth Gospel Camp.

This was the turning point in my life. In the camp, I was challenged about my beliefs. For the first time I realized that I was a sinner in need of forgiveness and salvation. I had always believed in God, but it was not enough. I thought I was already a Christian simply by belief in God's existence, but I was wrong. I really needed to repent and confess my sins before God. I tearfully prayed to God and asked him for forgiveness. Sincerely and truly I

asked Jesus to be Lord and Saviour. Although I was shy by nature, on the last day when an opportunity for individual testimony came, I bravely stood up, and very briefly said, "I've decided to be a true follower of Christ."

> The wind blows wherever it pleases. You hear its sound, but you cannot tell where it comes from or where it is going. So it is with everyone born of the Spirit (John 3:8).

This verse fully and vividly expresses my born again experience. I remember my school friends were amazed at the changes in me after the Summer vacation. Very often I had a pile of Gospel tracts in my school bag. I told all my friends about the experience of the Gospel camp, and asked them to consider believing in Jesus. Everybody knew that I had become a Christian!

Changed life

At home, my father was really puzzled. He did not understand what had happened to me as a result of the Summer camp. He obviously noticed that I had become 'different'. He watched me reading the Bible regularly every morning. Indeed, he knew too well that in the past I could hardly develop any kind of habit or hobby because of my lack of patience. He

probably thought that I would return to 'normal' after a couple of weeks! However, at first, he was quite pleased about the incredible changes in me.

A few months later, Father realized that I was actually very serious about my faith. He did not like me to be too involved in the church and Christianity. He became unhappy when I spent a lot of time in the church. Furthermore, because of my involvement in Sunday School and Christian fellowship, I began to spend less and less time at home. I felt that he was afraid or worried that one day I would love God more than him. Sometimes he could not hide his anger and hurt from me. I also began to sense the tension in our relationship.

I was very excited and full of joy as a new Christian. I enjoyed every opportunity to serve God and share the Gospel with people. I became very active in my church, Sunday School and school Christian fellowship. I even set up a small Bible Study group at home every Saturday afternoon. I was only a few months old spiritually, I hardly knew anything about the Bible, but I really desired to tell people about Jesus. Only three friends from school came regularly. Every time I simply read to them the sermon from the previous Sunday service. Of course, they did not know that the sermon was

from my church Sunday service! Only my father knew about it, but he was not allowed to come into my bedroom when I had the Bible Study meeting on Saturdays.

I persuaded them to come to church and Sunday School with me. Two years later, I was overwhelmed with joy when they accepted Jesus and became church members. Moreover, each of them stood firm through hardship and persecution because of their faith in Christ. To many Chinese people and families, Christianity was still regarded as a western religion and foreign to our culture and traditions. It was a very painful experience for my friends when they decided to be disciples of Christ.

I also experienced trouble myself, when my father tried to stop me attending church meetings, and having any contact with Christians. Once, it was really heartbreaking and difficult for us both when he asked me to make a choice between God and him. I remember he was so hurt that his voice was broken. He could not say a word, and his frail body was shaken because of anger and pain. We both had tears in our eyes.

Father was in his late sixties (I was worried about his health) and I was still in my teens. I knew that he had been seeing the doctor although he did not tell me. I was so afraid that one day he would die and leave me on my own.

I prayed for his salvation. I realized that he had no understanding of the Gospel even though he went to church regularly. About a year after I made my commitment to the Lord, I shared with him what I learned from my Bible study. Although he softened spiritually, he was still deeply hurt when I explained to him that I could no longer burn incense and say prayers to my mother.

Children obey your parents in the Lord, for this is right (Ephesians 6:1).

This verse came like a flash of brilliant light when I was struggling painfully with the question: 'How should I honour my father and mother and be right to God at the same time?' I realized that I should obey my father 'in the Lord', i.e. according to the Scripture. I also understood that everything 'in the Lord' would be everlasting. I very much wanted my love for Father to be an eternal one. It was very hard for me to admit that his heart condition had deteriorated over the months. I knew that he was dying. My earnest prayer was that Father would leave the world with the assurance of Christ's salvation. I continued to witness to him during the last year of his life and he realized that I still loved him very much. In the end, he found true peace in the Lord. My prayer was answered.

Burdened to serve God's people

Six months before Father passed away, there was another turning point in my life! I prayed to God, "Lord, if you want me to bring the Gospel back to your people then I will." I began to dream about a missionary's life in remote and far away places. I decided that my goal would be to take the Gospel back to Israel! I was one-and-a-half-years-old spiritually, still in my teens. I was young and maybe childish, but my prayer was truly sincere. I wanted to serve God and be part of his plan of salvation for the world. I made my commitment to this work one Sunday.

> But you will receive power when the Holy Spirit comes on you; and you will be my witnesses in Jerusalem, and in all Judea and Samaria, and to the ends of the earth (Acts 1:8).

> And so all Israel will be saved, as it is written: 'The deliverer will come from Zion; he will turn godlessness away from Jacob. And this is my covenant with them when I take away their sins' (Romans 11:26,27).

They were the main verses of the morning service. Through those verses and the challenging sermon, I committed myself to the service of the Jewish people. At that time I thought Jewish people lived in Israel only!

However, I did not tell anyone about my little, silent prayer that one day I would be a

missionary in Israel; it was my secret. After all, I had never heard anything about Israel, the chosen people. I really did wonder if Israel was still in existence, and if all Jewish people knew about the Gospel! Nobody I knew mentioned Israel. I did not tell people about my 'secret' because I was not sure how they would respond and react to me. If I had told people about my desire at that time, they probably would have thought that I was incredibly naive, or maybe out of my mind.

I needed to prepare myself for future service. My first training place was the home of my pastor. After the death of my father, my pastor and his wife invited me to stay with them in the church. I lived with my pastor's family for three years. I was like an extremely rough and ugly stone which needed a lot of polishing, moulding and shaping. It was not an easy time. But I continued to taste and experience God's mercy and goodness so abundantly.

I was given many opportunities to serve God in the church and in my school's Christian fellowship. Furthermore, I thought that everybody in the world outside Hong Kong spoke English only! I needed to study and improve my English. Hence, every day and night I prayed earnestly that I could continue my studies overseas. I was very eager to take every opportunity

of preparing myself for my goal. Eventually I succeeded.

In England, I completed my high school and Bible College education. After this, I worked in my home church in Hong Kong for two years. My desire to bring the Gospel to the Jewish people continued to grow stronger and stronger. One day I thought to myself, "If I can't be a missionary in the Land, I can still be a missionary in prayer." Therefore subsequently I wrote to all the mission organizations working in the Middle East according to a list of addresses in the book, *Operation World*. I asked them for prayer requests for Jewish Mission. But all of them replied that they only worked amongst Muslim people. However, one mission passed my letter on to *Christian Witness to Israel*. The Mission secretary replied to my letter. I then met the Director, Rev. M.A. MacLeod, in Hong Kong and I applied to the Mission in England.

My pastor told me, "When I was baptised in Shaihang, there were one hundred and three people baptised with me. Three of them were Jewish. My pastor baptised the three Jewish people first because the Scripture says, 'First to the Jews.'" He encouraged me when I talked to him about my desire to bring the Gospel to the Jewish people.

Arrives in London

I was in a panic! I arrived at London's Heathrow International Airport with tremendous enthusiasm and great expectancy on 26th September, 1982. I remembered that people told me that Jewish people could be recognized quite easily because they had longer and bigger noses. I looked around curiously and searched for Jewish faces amongst the big crowd in the airport, but everybody's nose seemed to be longer and bigger than my Chinese nose! "Where are the Jewish people? How am I going to find them?" I worried.

* * * * * *

Giving out tracts at the High Street in Stamford Hill (a Jewish area in N. London), I was very much aware of the hostility of the ultra-orthodox Jewish people. A furious-looking elderly Jewish man came towards me. He grabbed the Gospel tract in my hand, and tore it into pieces. Then he wanted to hit me. I noticed a scar with numbers on his arm. He was obviously a victim of anti-Semitism and probably had been in a Nazi concentration camp. I ran to my colleague for help.

> I am not ashamed of the gospel, because it is the power of God for the salvation of everyone who believes: first for the Jew, then for the Gentile.

20

This verse from Romans 1:16 came to my mind as later I reflected on the whole incident. I admit that I could only begin to understand what Paul was talking about in that verse. Although I had heard many powerful sermons on Romans 1:16, the experience of it struck me so immensely that I would never forget what Paul meant by 'I am not ashamed of the Gospel'.

I believe that the Gospel is the power of God for the salvation of everyone who believes: first for the Jew, then for the Gentile. I have been working among the Jewish people in London for over seven years. The first two years were especially difficult as I had to find ways of reaching out to the Jewish community. I did mostly door-to-door visitation and giving out tracts in Jewish areas. I attended Hebrew classes. I found the learning of Jewish culture and Jewish history most interesting and fascinating. Yet, on the other hand, at times I felt so inadequate and weak in my approach to Jewish evangelism. It is truly the power of God, which alone can 'open doors' and enable me to bring the Gospel to the Jewish people.

"We are Jewish!" This is the common response to door-to-door work. To become a Christian is to go across to the other side and become a traitor to your own people. "If I become a Christian, my mother will be so sad..."

"If I become a Christian, my father will kill himself..." These are some of my Jewish friends' responses. It takes years of patience and perseverance to build up a trusting relationship, where one can frankly and freely share, discuss and talk about matters of faith. The patient, daily witness of one Christian neighbour led to this powerful testimony: "I became a Christian because 'Jesus' lives next door to me!"

There is no greater joy than helping someone to find new life in Jesus the Messiah. It is indeed by grace that I am 'chosen' to have a part in his service, as he says:

> 'You did not choose me, but I chose you to go and bear fruit - fruit that will last' (John 15:16).

I long to see many Jewish people coming to acknowledge Jesus as their Messiah. God is still working out the salvation of everyone who believes: first for the Jew, then for the Gentile. He never ceases to fulfil his promises to his people. He must keep his covenant with his ancient people.

* * * * * *

No, I am no longer 'a daughter of Kun-Yan' but of the living God!

Praise be to the God and Father of our Lord Jesus Christ, who has blessed us in the heavenly realms with every spiritual blessing in Christ. For he chose us in him before the creation of the world to be holy and blameless in his sight. In love he predestined us to be adopted as his sons through Jesus Christ, in accordance with his pleasure and will - to the praise of his glorious grace, which he has freely given us in the One he loves (Ephesians 1:3-6).

Therefore, God has also made me an heir:

Because you are sons, God sent the Spirit of his Son into our hearts, the Spirit who calls out, 'Abba Father.' So you are no longer a slave, but a son (Galatians 4:6,7).

God has set me free to serve him. Indeed, salvation has come to me, to the Chinese people, to the Gentiles to make Israel envious (Romans 11:11).

2

He Found Me - J. Douglas MacMillan

I was born in the County of Argyll, in the Parish of Western Ardnamurchan on the last day of September, 1933. I had the great privilege of being born into a Christian home and was the youngest of six children, two girls and four boys. The most westerly point of mainland Britain, Ardnamurchan is a peninsula running out into the Atlantic ocean with the island of Skye lying to the North and the island of Mull to the South. It was, in many ways, an idyllic place in which to be brought up and fostered in me a great love for the countryside, and in particular, the sea and the mountains.

When I was a little boy, my father was a building-contractor but also ran a croft, or small farm on which the family did the work. From the earliest time I can remember, the croft animals, cows and calves, sheep and lambs, horses, and, of course, collie dogs were part of our rich and varied everyday life. We did not realise it at the time, but it was a kind of life fast fading into the obscurity of history.

My father was a very hard-working, upright,

honest, able man with a fine mind and a very skilful pair of hands. A deeply exercised Christian, his heart was open to all kinds of people and he was a helper of every needy person and cause. I don't think I have ever met anyone whom I have respected in quite the same way as I respected him. He was converted in middle life, in the year 1921, when a visiting preacher held meetings in our village. He went through a long, trying period under great conviction of sin and was hugely troubled for a time over the doctrine of election. His deliverance from all this came by way of a powerful experience of God's grace in Christ when reading a sermon on that very subject by C. H. Spurgeon.

I have counted it as a fortunate thing that, being the son of a bardic family and endowed with a fine command of good, fluent Gaelic, he has left some of his early spiritual experiences on record in the form of a few fine Gaelic spiritual songs and hymns. After his conversion he, himself, began to preach and along with other young Christian converts of that period to hold Cottage meetings in the villages surrounding his home. My mother, Jessie MacLachlan, was also of Ardnamurchan people on both sides of her family, but had been born and brought up in Glasgow. She came to Ardnamurchan to care for an elderly uncle and

soon afterwards was converted through hearing my father preach.

Memories of my childhood are happy ones and many of them centre around the gospel and the love which the gospel always brings into a home. I still recall very vividly our worship times as a family, my father's prayers, and his carrying me on his shoulders as we went through the woods and over the hill tracks to the lovely, white-sanded bay where the people of four little hamlets met for worship and preaching at three o'clock on Sunday afternoons. Our home often entertained the preachers or other Christians and so I think I always knew that the Lord's people were happy and greatly enjoyed each others' fellowship.

I remember, on one occasion, sitting in that small church at Sanna Bay listening to our minister preaching on the Judgment and describing how people on that Day would call on the mountains to fall on them and cover them from the face of God. At one point in his sermon, he tip-toed, very gently, over to the windows of this little church and, pointing upwards to where we could all see the huge, rugged, granite rocks and boulders perched on the steep slopes of the hills as they towered above us, he said, in a voice filled in awe, "People will be calling on those very rocks and

hills to hide them from God, if they are not ready to meet him on that great day." I was probably only three or four years old at the time, but I can still remember feeling the power of that moment and the still, solemn hush that came over us all.

I can remember something else which had an even more vivid and lasting effect on my life and which took place when I was eight years old. In our times of family worship we used to sing some verses of a Psalm; and, one Sunday evening when we were singing the opening verses of Psalm 40 I had a very powerful sense of the nearness, and the love of God. As we sang, I felt something very special in these words which speak about God taking us out of the miry clay, setting our feet upon a rock, and putting a new song in our mouths. My heart was touched and melted, and I really felt that God loved me and had come to me and so I told my parents and my friends at school that I had been converted. For quite a long time after I tried to live like a Christian, at home and at school.

Outgrowing religion

When I was nearly twelve I had to leave home to attend secondary school at Tobermory, on the island of Mull. Here, two things worked against me continuing to think and act as a

Christian. First of all, there were no other believers of my own age. Secondly, one of my new teachers positively undermined my faith in the Bible. By the time I was thirteen, I felt I had outgrown religion. I put behind me the impressions I had had from early childhood. Religion was all right for the likes of my parents, whom I regarded as old and old-fashioned, but it was not something which I needed.

Before I was fourteen, I had to leave school. Two years earlier my father had moved to quite a large farm which he ran with my two older brothers and, at certain times, help from an uncle with the sheep. My oldest brother was leaving home that Autumn to study at Veterinary College in Glasgow and, at the same time, I ran into difficulties finding accommodation near my school. Just as these were being overcome, in the month of January 1948, my uncle died very suddenly and so with pressure of work in looking after his croft with its horse, cows and sheep, as well as the sheep on our own farm, I was, to my own entire satisfaction, allowed to abandon any further thought of returning to school almost a year before attaining the minimum leaving age and, in the event, never went back at all.

I had just got settled into this new situation and the beginning of a working teenage life

when my mother, who had had surgery a year or so earlier, began to be very unwell and finally became ill with a painful, terminal cancer. Strangely enough, despite her own faith and cheerfulness, her illness and especially the long, dragged-out, closing year of her life confirmed me in the anti-religious, anti-Christian mental attitudes I had begun to adopt during my last year at school.

Another influence in my life at this time was the books I used to borrow from a man with communist views (a red Clydesider) who came to live not far away. As I read these books, especially through the long wintry nights, I felt confirmed in my rejection of Christianity.

Will I meet you in Heaven?

I also recall something which happened one night in the early Springtime of that final year of mother's life. My brother and I had been out at a ceilidh and dance, singing and playing accordions in a village about thirty-five miles away. We got home in the wee, small hours of the morning - just as a new day was beginning to break. I opened the back door of our house and immediately heard a strange, but beautiful sound. It was my mother's voice. She had had some training in voice production when young and had, at one time, sung with some groups in

Glasgow. But here she was now, just months before her death and at a time when her days were often filled with great pain, awake in the middle of the night with the stress of her illness, and my father sitting with her, softly singing a glorious testimony of faith in the verses of one of her favourite Psalms:

> I shall not die, but live, and shall
> The works of God discover:
> The Lord hath me chastised sore,
> But not to death giv'n over.
>
> O set ye open unto me
> The gates of righteousness;
> Then will I enter into them,
> And I the Lord will bless.   (Psalm 118: 17-19)

She was singing the second verse just as my hand was on the handle of the back door. I was so overcome I could not go in. I went away up into the hills to cry. Here I was full of youthfulness and with everything opening out before me, and there she was, so weak and in such pain, yet singing with triumph about what was opening out before her. There was something about that, and about her whole life, that touched even my hard heart.

Three months later, one hot day in July, I was in my mother's room and she asked me to read a few verses for her from the Bible.

"Where would you like me to read?"

"In John chapter 14."

I took up the Bible and began to read:

Let not your heart be troubled: ye believe in God, believe also in me. In my Father's house are many mansions: if it were not so, I would have told you. I go to prepare a place for you. And if I go and prepare a place for you, I will come again, and receive you unto myself; that where I am, there ye may be also.

"That's enough."

"But, Mam, would you not like me to read a bit more? I could read the whole chapter." (I was actually feeling quite proud that I could do this for my mother.)

But she said, "No, Douglas, that's enough. That's everything." Then she turned to me and said, "Douglas, there is something I want to say to you. I may never talk to you again. In a short time I am going to be with Jesus. But I want to ask you, *Will you meet me there?*"

Four days later, she died. So seven days after that last conversation, I was standing beside my mother's grave. It was as if I could hear her voice ringing in my ears, 'Will I meet you in Heaven?' I knew that, if there was a Heaven, I was not walking on the road that led to it. I felt I had to harden my heart against my mother's appeal, and I did.

Were you in church last Sunday?

However, there were many things which began to get to me and leave me very uneasy with my life and outlook. For example, in my work as a shepherd I was closely in touch with nature. Especially in lambing time I had to get up when it was dark and climb the hills as day was dawning. From the height of the mountains behind our house, the beauty of nature was staggering. I remember sitting down on the top of a mountain, early one morning, and looking out to the west. I could see the nearer islands and beyond them, the Outer Hebrides. Beyond that, there was nothing between me and America. The beauty and immensity of everything made my hair stand on end. I could not get the question out of my head - *Where did all this come from*?

To cut a long story short, six or seven years of atheism came to an end as I found it actually easier to accept the existence of God than to go on believing that all this beauty and order came from nothing.

But now a new struggle started. What if the God who made the world was the same God as my parents believed in? What if the Bible was true? What if there was a Heaven and a Hell? I remember that, as I was out drinking one evening, I was suddenly overcome by the seriousness of a question from which I could not

escape. *What if all I had been taught about the Bible was true?*

One night, when I was in a local pub, a man asked me, "Douglas, were you in church last Sunday?"

I said, "No - not me! These fellows just put me to sleep."

A week later I was playing my accordion at a dance. I got up to dance with a girl and, as we moved round the floor together, she suddenly asked me, "Douglas, were you in church last Sunday?" I was beginning to feel persecuted! But she went on: "There's a wonderful young preacher. You must go and hear him." I'll not repeat what I said to her.

The mask removed

My older brother used to drive my father to the mid-week service in the church six or seven miles away. But one Wednesday around that time my brother was away at a cattle sale and I got the job of driving my father to the church. I intended, while he was in the church, going to the pub for a drink and then going to visit a girl. However, as we came near to the church I had an idea. I asked my father, "Who will be preaching tonight? Is it that young preacher?"

"Yes."

I thought, "This is my chance to find out what

they are all talking about." I went in with my father, but as soon as I sat down in the church amongst these old people I began to wonder if I was going mad. What if my mates found out that I spent my Wednesday evening in a church!

Then the door behind the pulpit opened and I got quite a shock. I thought that all preachers were old men, ready to crumble and fall into the grave. They were religious because there was nothing better for them to do. But this young man was just a little older than I was myself. He looked as if he had a broken nose - in fact his whole appearance reminded me of my hero - Freddie Mills, the British cruiserweight boxer who was then champion of the world.

At first I was disappointed when he began to speak. His voice was low, as if he was afraid of all the old ladies in black. His text was:

> Because thou sayest, I am rich, and increased in goods, and have need of nothing; and knowest not that you are wretched, and miserable, and poor, and blind and naked: I counsel you to buy from me gold tried in the fire... (Revelation 3:17-18).

To this day I am amazed that he chose to speak on a text like that when he must have expected to address a group of old Christians. Anyway he described what he found in the text - the spectacle of a soul worshipping itself.

What took my breath away was - he gave an exact description of me, and of my life. I was living for myself, for pleasure and for what I could accomplish. I drank, I enjoyed the company of the lassies, but there were also hard ambitions which had taken over my life. I lived for money, and there was another thing. I used to do the round of the Highland Games, and often featured in the prize lists for the 'Heavy Events'. I was especially keen on hammer throwing. I had been doing it since I was fifteen and thought that in about four years I could reach the top.

But, as I listened to the preacher in that quiet country church, all these things lost their dazzle. The very things which had become the focal point for my driving ambition began suddenly to look pathetic and empty. What was the point in giving over my life to these things? The mask was being removed from my life.

I began to wonder - "Did my old man tell this preacher about me? But no; I did not even know myself I would be listening to this until I stopped at the door."

I was not converted that night, though I promised the preacher that I would come to church again. It was three weeks before I saw him. I was driving along beside the sea in the old lorry we used at the farm when I spotted him

walking beside the road, carrying a Calor gas cylinder. He had about a mile to go yet. I said to myself, "Will I stop, or will I go roaring past him? If I give him a lift, he'll ask me why I haven't been back in church." In the end I stopped and said quite roughly to him, "Want a lift, Jock?" He wanted a lift all right. He threw the cylinder in the back and climbed up beside me. Just as I thought, the first thing he said to me was, "You never came back to church."

"No - I've been busy."

"You are a liar."

"That's a terrible thing for a preacher to say."

"But you are a liar; it wasn't because you were busy - am I right?"

"I suppose you are."

He shouted, above the sound of the old engine, "You know what I think? I think you are running scared. I think you are scared that you will get converted."

"No, I am not scared. Actually, I would like to be converted, but I don't think I can be."

"What do you mean?"

"Well, since that night, I have asked God two or three times to convert me and nothing has happened."

By this time we had reached where he was staying. He said, "Why don't you come in?"

It can't be as simple as that!

I went in with him, and he talked to me as no-one had ever talked before. Then he said to me, "If you are really serious about this, what about going down on your knees and we will ask God to change you."

I wasn't very keen. I was embarrassed, but then I said to myself, "I want this if I can get it," so I went down on my knees. At first he wanted me to pray but there was no way I was going to do that with him there. I said, "You are the one who is paid to do the praying. You pray!"

He began to talk to God as if he really knew him and as he continued he quoted John 3:16:

> God so loved the world that he gave his only begotten Son, that whosoever believeth in him should not perish but have everlasting life.

I had known these words all my life, but as he quoted them it was as if someone drew aside curtains so that light came into a dark room. I understood these words in a new way. I saw that Christ had finished all that was necessary for my salvation. I didn't have to do anything to save my soul. I got a hold of the preacher's arm and said, "Say that again."

He stared at me. "Say what again?"

"That bit about God loving the world: say that again."

He repeated the text.

I said, "Does that mean that, if I really believe that Jesus is the Son of God and that he died on the Cross at Calvary to save us from our sins, and trust him because of that, I will be saved?"

He said, "Yes - that's just what it means."

I said, "It can't be as simple as that!"

But, although I was arguing like that, I felt I was understanding the way of salvation for the first time in my life. What I had known in one way for so long now seemed so new! And as I believed it for the first time, a great peace began to flood into my heart, and a stillness came over me.

Then I thought, "That's all right, but you know how a Christian is supposed to live." I began thinking of all the things I would have to stop. He saw my face changing and asked, "What's wrong now?"

I said, "I don't think I could live like a Christian. I would have to give up too much."

"Listen, Douglas," he said. "You think through everything you feel you would have to give up. Think about it very carefully." Then he said, "In this hand, (holding out his right hand) I'll give you everything you are afraid of losing; and in this hand (holding out his left hand) I'll give you Christ."

He didn't make it easy for me. I'm sure I must have sat there for ten minutes (he said afterwards it felt like an eternity) thinking deeply about all that was involved. Then at last I absolutely knew which one I had to take. I said, "If I can really have Christ as my Saviour, I'll take him." As soon as I had said that, my heart was filled with joy and love.

Then I suddenly remembered my father. I had dropped him off in the village at two o'clock. He was going to collect his pension and visit a friend, and I was to have picked him up at four o'clock. By this time it was twenty past seven. I said to the preacher, "Man, I've forgotten my old man. He has been waiting on me for three and a half hours."

I jumped into the old lorry and went roaring off back to the little bungalow where my father had said he would be. The lady came to the door and let me in. I hurried ahead of her into the living room. My father was sitting opposite the door. As soon as I came in he got up, crossed the room, took me in his arms and said, "Douglas, thank God."

"Why?"

"You've been converted."

"How do you know?"

"I could see in you face, as soon as you came in the door, that my prayers had been answered."

Call to the ministry

By the time I had been a Christian for two years I was quite sure that the Lord was calling me to preach the gospel. I tried to satisfy this demanding heart-urge by applying for, and getting acceptance as a Lay Preacher with my local Presbytery. Having spoken at one or two of the little, weekly Prayer Meetings conducted by my father, I preached my first sermon in Lochgilphead Free Church, in March 1957. My father died in June of that year and it was in the days following that momentous - but in some ways marvellous - event, I knew that I would have to seek entrance to the ministry of the gospel.

At end of August 1958, I left home to take up full time study at Skerrys' College, Edinburgh, with a view to entering the ministry of the Free Church of Scotland. I had, of course, at least four years of secondary school studies to make up and knew that I was facing an uphill task. Over the next two years, my time was spent in studying for University Preliminary Entrance exams.

My only source of income, once I stopped work, was an annual grant of £70 from the church so, to make ends meet, I drove a lorry in the afternoons for a Haulier who used to camp on our farm over the Summer holidays. He and his wife and family were tremendously kind to

me at that time and were a great help during a period when I felt very homesick and missed my dogs, my sheep and my hills.

Throughout that period, though, the Lord was really good to me. I enjoyed listening to fine preaching, made many new Christian friends and, within two years, gained passes which enabled me to enter Aberdeen University. I enjoyed my time there enormously, marrying at the end of my first Session, and graduating MA in 1963. I then returned to Edinburgh to pursue my theological studies at the Free Church College.

Places of service

I was ordained to the gospel ministry, and inducted to my first pastorate in St Columba Free Church, Aberdeen, on 3rd September, 1966. The congregation was not large but both Mary and I knew it well from our student days and over the last few years of my predecessor's very faithful ministry it had not only grown in numbers but it had increased in spiritual vigour as well and there was a fine tone and quality to its life. We knew that during the University Sessions there would be quite a number of students amongst us.

During my time in the Dee Street Church, as it was most popularly known, my ministry was

quite varied with a lot of hospital visiting, evangelism amongst lapsed church-goers, open-air meetings, street tracting and work amongst College and University students. We saw the Lord at work amongst the people there and over the years quite a number of young people were converted. This was one of the happiest periods of my life and I enjoyed the work tremendously. I was quite heart-broken when I felt the time had come to leave for another church.

In 1974 I was given, and after much heart-searching, accepted a call to St Vincent Street Free Church in Glasgow. The work there was different from Aberdeen but I also enjoyed it a great deal. There I saw quite a number of older people being converted - indeed, the first person and the last which I knew to be definitely converted to Christ there were both over seventy years of age, something which I had always regarded as quite unusual. Anyway, I ministered very happily there until 1982 when I was appointed to the chair of Church History and Church Principles in the Free Church College, Edinburgh.

I had eight years at the College and much enjoyed working with the men studying for the ministry of our own and various other churches. I was able to speak and preach in many places

outwith Scotland and came to know the Lord's work on a wider scale than formerly.

I had just indicated acceptance of a call to a congregation in Edinburgh, where I am now ministering, when I took ill with coronary disease in the late Spring of 1990. That eventuated in open heart surgery and a triple by-pass in July of that year. It was my first ever experience of hospital or of serious illness and it is a great joy for me to say that through all this rather traumatic experience I was very deeply aware of the Saviour's presence and felt my heart fortified by his peace.

I was very humbled by the huge number of calls and letters we received - from all around the world, almost - assuring us of continued prayer both from churches and individuals. And those prayers were wonderfully answered. It was a marvellous experience to feel myself absolutely cushioned with the love and power of Christ on the evening before my operation and not merely to know, but actually to feel that I was on the receiving end of a huge battery of Christian love and Christian prayer.

Over the months since then, I have made steady progress back to health and have been able to pick up the beginnings of a new ministry amongst a people from whom, and in whom, I receive many tokens of the Lord's love and

graciousness. On the medical side of things I have also received great kindness as well as dedicated and attentive care. I have marvelled at the skill, patience, and sheer professionalism of all the people involved in this ministry of healing and, under God, owe them a great deal.

Gratitude to God

I feel that I owe a special debt of gratitude to the Lord, for the help and support I have had from my wife, Mary, in our thirty years together as well as during this last year and its times of illness and utter weakness. As I have indicated, she is also a graduate of Aberdeen University, was a teacher prior to our marriage, and is the daughter of a well-known Free Church minister and writer, the late Rev Murdoch Campbell, Resolis. Mary has been a great help right through my ministry and has made our home a place where people feel welcome.

We have five children; Eilidh (Gaelic for Helen); Murdo; Mhairi (Mary); Neil and Douglas. All of them are grown up now and are deeply committed Christians. The first is a Social Worker in Inverness; the second works with the Department of Agriculture; the third is a Clinical Psychologist; the fourth is studying for the ministry of our church; and the youngest is a student in Cardiff.

Looking back over my life the greatest thing which ever happened to me was, without a shadow of a doubt, my conversion in 1955. I have never regretted that the Lord sought, and found me, a lost, unworthy sinner and changed my heart and life with his grace and power. The Lord has been very gracious and good to me down through the years, and has never failed me.

My only regrets lie along the line of my own many failures to be all that I should have been for him - but, despite the sins and disobedience and the imperfect service I have been able to give to the Lord I would not want to change any of it. My life has been full and happy, and every day has been rich with his love and mercy.

I would like to guard against the thought that I am in any way special, or that my experience, although so uniquely personal, is any different in principle from that of other Christians. It is not so. I am a very ordinary person who was found and saved by a very extraordinary Saviour, and I owe him a debt that can never be repaid either in this world or in the world to come. The wonder that filled my heart the night I first found Jesus in June 1955 is still there - the complete wonder that, as Paul put it long ago, *He loved me, and gave himself for me.*

3

He Found Me - Anne Rayment

Shortly after the end of the last war my father stepped on to the ferry at Dublin and began his journey to a new life on the other side of the Irish Sea. Like many of his fellow-countrymen before him he sought the wider opportunities for employment offered in England, and was prepared to work hard in order to better himself. Travelling south to London, he took on a variety of menial and labouring jobs before eventually obtaining a good position as a teacher and settling south of the Thames.

The family he left behind in Tipperary was respectable and middle-class, the sons of which were usually destined to the family business or the priesthood. They were wealthy enough to employ domestic staff but not so wealthy as to be idle themselves. Of course, they were Irish through and through, staunch supporters of the nationalist cause and unswervingly Catholic. Religion and politics were as inextricably linked in Ireland then as now, and resentment against the English (and consequently Protestantism) ran deep. Tales of misdeeds by the Anglo-

Saxon oppressors have been passed down through generations of my family and have an almost romantic flavour to them, particularly the one concerning the injustice perpetrated by Cromwell's henchmen who 'appropriated' our ancestral home, and the one about the family heroine who succoured victims of the Potato Famine. All of these stories are no doubt founded on fact, and served to reinforce the belief that to be truly Irish was to be Catholic.

Despite these inherited prejudices, my father married an English Protestant girl who did not object to sending their offspring to Catholic Schools or taking them to Mass on Sundays. There are a great many Catholics of Irish extraction in London, and as a result one could grow up in an environment quite isolated from Protestant England. I myself was educated in convent schools until the age of eighteen, and along with the Bernadettes and Philomenas of my generation, was denied no opportunity to practice the religion of my forebears. We would all take our first confession as a matter of course, followed soon by our first Holy Communion, and then by our confirmation. The local department store did a roaring trade in tiny white dresses and veils.

We were taught that to miss Mass was a sin and that we were equally obliged to go to

Church on certain appointed feasts known as 'Holy Days of Obligation'. We learned that the Seven Sacraments of the Church (from Baptism to Extreme Unction) were our path of salvation, and that we would all (unless we were saintly enough to be canonised) have to endure Purgatory on account of our sins before we could enter heaven. The remote, stern figure of God could be appealed to in prayer via the intercession of the more sympathetic Blessed Virgin Mary. Saints in heaven could also obtain forgiveness for us, but Jesus Christ was less accessible to us, somehow, than those mediators appointed by the Catholic Church.

We were taught respect for authority at home and at school. Irish parents of my father's generation were strict disciplinarians who could instil obedience through fear, and their children, as a result, behaved well with their teachers. Catholic schools boasted excellent exam records, and violence and vandalism were almost unheard of in my own convent grammar, as in others.

I cannot remember having heard the good news about Christ during those years of religious education and practice, but I was simply deaf to the gospel then, despite the fact that Bible readings were a part of every Mass. We were all given Catholic Revised Standard Ver-

sions of the Bible at school and encouraged to venerate the Word of God. These Bibles were studied in R.E. classes as we prepared to take our 'O' level in that subject. Most of us passed. We individualised our Bibles with stickers and doodles just as young evangelicals are often wont to do, only the Bibles of convent girls would be filled with picture cards of the saints, Our Lady and Our Lord rather than the motto-cards favoured by evangelicals. Christian Unions were unknown at school, and although we could all recite the 'Hail, Holy Queen' and tell our rosaries with ease, we never met to pray or share spiritual experiences. It did not occur to us to do so.

The attitude of my peers to religion at that time was, generally speaking, one of disdain, and we would blaspheme carelessly and miss Mass, Confession and Holy Days whenever possible. We respected the nuns and did not mock their devotion, but would not want to be so unfashionable as to be 'religious' ourselves. Like most teenagers we rebelled against all forms of authority, but like most teenagers our rebelliousness was only skin-deep. In later life we would calm down, appreciate the merits of our background, and seek to reproduce in ourselves the virtues once despised in our elders.

Thus it was that in my middle twenties, after

a few years of religious backsliding, I began to want to get back to my roots. My religious observance from my late teens until then had been erratic, but after marriage and the birth of my first child I determined to pick up the habit once more. I wanted my children to learn about God and to adopt the moral principles I valued, and I felt that in order to achieve this I had to be a convincing Christian myself.

My husband happily tolerated my Mass-going, but was not disposed to adopt the practice himself, having no spiritual inclinations of his own, coming from a nominal 'chapel' background. Nevertheless, he would often patiently accompany me to services, in spite of the fact that he derived less from the experience than I did.

Contentedly, then, for a time, I attended the Sacraments, but although this gave me some satisfaction, I was dismayed to find that the more I heard about Christianity, the more I discovered my doubts. My unease increased to the point where merely to recite the Creed was no longer enough. Surely I had to believe at least most of the points of doctrine, or my declaration was a sham. There was no worth in knowing the words if I did not fully endorse their meaning.

Did I really believe that God was a God of

love? Did I really believe he governed the affairs of men? Could I really, wholeheartedly, accept the authority of the Pope and obey his every command? Did the Virgin Mary really hear me when I prayed? Why was Jesus such a dark mystery when he was supposed to be the axis of my faith?

Something deep inside me told me that Christianity was true, and that the truth about God was to be found somewhere within Christianity. The problem for me, however, was that I had to find this absolute, eternal truth for myself without knowing exactly where to find it. Did the priests have the answers, or did the Bible, or was assurance never to be found? The *faith of my fathers'* was not enough: I had to have *my faith*. Something from God could set my soul on fire - but what was it? It was no longer enough to have a vague inner feeling that Christianity was true: I had to be able to defend that inner feeling with real conviction. I had to know, not just to sense. The Christian martyrs of the church calendar must have had more than just a 'sense', or they would not have been prepared to die for their faith.

If I could not find whatever it was I was looking for, I could no longer keep up a pretence of belief. I was either a whole-hearted Christian or an atheist, and if I was an atheist I

51

would cease attending Mass. Looking back now, I can see this spiritual crisis as a turning point. Looking back, I can see that this was the beginning of God's pull on me.

From here on events took an almost uncanny turn. My husband's brother, Richard, suddenly started to 'get religious'. He had never been religious before, but now he enthused about God and spiritual things in a way that astounded us. His personality altered in a remarkable and favourable way, and it was obvious to my husband Chas and me that something had happened within him. He seemed so unusually happy and at peace, but without any change of outward circumstances. It was as if he were a new person. Something fascinating radiated from him. What was it? Whatever it was drew me.

Richard gave me little booklets of what I would now describe as of an evangelistic nature. I read them with interest, and something else of great significance occurred that made me read them all the more.

A friend introduced me to some members of an evangelical church, and I attended a few of their women's meetings. Never before had I encountered such people as these, and I was amazed at them, for I knew almost at once that they possessed the elusive treasure I had been

seeking: that real faith that moves people. God and Jesus Christ were alive to these women in the same way that God and Jesus Christ were alive to Richard, and not to Chas and me. There was a connection between the faith of these women and that of Richard's, and I knew that clues as to its nature were contained in those leaflets at home.

I read on, struggling to understand and burning with questions. Having by no means abandoned my Catholicism, I took my burning questions to the parish priest.

I asked him why it was that the Pope was infallible, and I asked him whether the Bible was a reliable source of information regarding theology. I asked him if it were true that Protestants were all inevitably hell-bound, as I had been taught to believe. The Protestant denial of transubstantiation was a major stumbling-block to me at that time, and I asked the priest to explain the Catholic Church's reasons for believing that the bread and wine on the altar became the actual body and blood of Christ.

The priest was glad to explain to me all these matters and assured me of the usefulness of Scripture. He told me that it was the Word of God and, as such, venerable. Papal infallibility and transubstantiation he justified using verses of the New Testament, and I was satisfied with

his exegesis. He said that he, personally, did not consider all Protestants automatically doomed to hell, and that Protestants were our brothers and sisters in Christ. This comforted me, as did his tolerance of my growing association with Protestants after I confessed to having been to a service at my 'new' evangelical church. The priest saw no reason why I should not attend the occasional Sunday service with non-Catholics provided I compensated for it by also attending Mass the same day. This compromise I considered most reasonable, and readily agreed to follow the priest's instruction. I left the presbytery with a copy of Leo Treze's *The Faith Explained* (loaned to me by the priest as it contained further 'proofs' of transubstantiation) and went my way content.

In my heart of hearts, however, I knew that I was still in a crisis. I knew that my current division of denominational loyalties was a betrayal of both camps. One day I would have to decide where I belonged, for I could not attend both churches indefinitely. I would have to make up my mind.

The question of Holy Communion really bogged me down. I could quite understand the Catholic view that the communion wafer was the true body of Christ made palatable, but I could equally appreciate the Protestant view

that the wafer or bread was symbolic. Both schools of thought justified their position with the same verses of Scripture, and both views sounded to me to be equally reasonable. I knew that transubstantiation was an important issue for both denominations, and that I had to decide whom to believe, and yet I was frustrated and bewildered because I knew I did not have the knowledge to make an intelligent judgment on the matter. I was no theologian - how could I sort out such a difficult problem? In retrospect now, I can see that at the time I was allowing myself to be distracted from my main quest.

I became more and more involved in the evangelical church, at the expense of the Catholic one. I became a regular attender at Sunday services and found, to my regret, that the Mass suffered greatly by comparison. Why was that? I think it was because the service seemed so full of life compared to the Mass. The service had a certain energy and vitality that made me sit up and take notice, whereas the Mass seemed to be all ceremony and liturgy. The service had a relevance and immediacy, whereas the Mass seemed detached from reality. The preacher at the service had a message for me, whereas the priest's sermon sounded non-specific and generalised. The congregation in the service were

attentive and contributive, whereas the congregation at Mass appeared uninterested and passive. I knew these differences were more than differences of style.

During this time of searching, understanding dawned for me, leading me towards my spiritual goal, until ultimately the goal itself became clear. Looking back now, I can see that I was not searching at all, but that God was leading me on to a destination prepared in advance not only for me, but also for my family.

Something astonishing began to happen as I read my Bible and listened to the preaching at the evangelical church. Gradually, over a period of a few weeks, something became revealed to me that was new, surprising, and of life-changing importance.

That 'something' was of greater significance to me than the answers to my questions about Papal infallibility and other doctrinal differences between Protestants and Catholics. It was far more important even than the vexed problem of transubstantiation. In fact, in the blazing light of what was now revealed to me, all my puzzlings appeared suddenly pedantic, small, and of very little consequence whatsoever. I forgot to worry about which denomination held the monopoly on truth as Jesus Christ himself came into sharp focus for the very first time.

The Son of God shone out from the pages of the Bible as he had done all along, but unperceived until now. The words of Scripture had been as if in an unknown language, but were now at last comprehensible, their message as loud and clear as a newspaper headline.

Jesus Christ was no longer a shadowy, forbidding herald of God's judgment, standing aloof from sinners in the unapproachable vaults of heaven. Neither was he a weak, defeated dogooder, sad of countenance and limp of hand.

The Christ I now knew stood strong and full of power, bold and uncompromising, the mouthpiece of God, declaring his wrath and his commandments in the same firm, level tone of voice that assured me of his mercy and compassion. Christ's voice rang out from the pages of the New Testament telling me, as he had always done, who he was and what he had done for mankind. For the first time, I listened to him say he was alive today and was God's bearer of salvation to all who put their trust in him.

I heard him tell me that Calvary was a place of victory where all my sins, even those I had yet to commit, found their atonement. I heard him invite all people to fellowship with him, and through him to peace with God the Father. I heard him tell me that my sins were more than just a blot on my conscience: my sins had alien-

ated me from God. But Christ also told me that the same God of eternal judgment had also provided the only means of reconciliation - in the Lord Jesus Christ himself. Christ had suffered the punishment that was due to me. He had sacrificed himself in my place so that I could draw near to God. Without forgiveness of my sins, through Christ, I would never see heaven.

How strange that through all my years of gazing at crucifixes I had never, until that time, really appreciated what the crucifixion meant! The cross had been linked to Christ in much the same way that Our Lady always dressed in blue: it was his accessory. I had never fully understood Calvary's purpose!

As this amazing information came home to me, my doubts and spiritual worries fell away. I earnestly committed myself in prayer to that which I now understood, and emerged, eternally relieved, into the dawn of a new day. It was as if the world had been re-created: everything I now observed around me was illuminated by the light of Christ. My attitudes changed, my values changed, and my outlook on life changed forever. At last I had found what I was looking for.

I was far too interested now in my relationship with God to concern myself with transubstantiation and Papal infallibility, and I simply

ceased to be troubled by those questions. It was only years later that I returned to them, resumed my research, and sorted out my views.

I ceased attending the Catholic church altogether, and actually broke away from my old ways very easily, suffering no pangs of guilt or doubt at all. Having discovered the place where the truth of God was proclaimed, nothing else now had any hold on me. Once assured of my place with God in heaven, how could I fear excommunication and rejection by other mortals?

When I told my evangelical friends that I had come to an understanding of Christ's work in salvation I discovered they had been praying I should do so all along. Richard also had been concerned for me and was thankful to God that I had come to faith.

What of my husband? Chas's own attitude to his relationship with God was beginning to change in response to God's leading. His interest in the subject matter of religious tracts started to gain a new intensity, and he became troubled about the state of his soul. Roughly five months after my own conversion, he too was challenged by God to the point where he could no longer resist, and surrendered to the truth. He too was now born again, and we were baptized together after the practice of our church. Our family life

now had a radically new basis, and we could bring up our children in the love and fear of the Lord.

Parent-child relationships in my parental home, however, suffered a downward turn. I felt it a privilege and a necessary duty to share my new-found faith with my father, but predicted that to do so would be no easy task. I was right.

I stated my case to him quite clearly, willing him to appreciate the sincerity of my convictions while hastening to assure him that I in no wise disdained the sound moral education imparted to me via Catholicism. In truth, I have only gratitude to that church for teaching me the respect for authority, consideration of others, self-discipline and self-examination that are vital to any Christian's faith. I thought no less of the nuns who had guided me than I ever had done, and in fact I appreciated more than ever their devotion to, and love for, God.

My father, unfortunately, was not sympathetic, and could not perceive of anything beyond the sectarian struggles of his forbears. Religion was to him a matter of loyalties: one was either 'orange' or a 'teague'. Purely spiritual matters were to him an irrelevance. In his eyes, I had sided with the 'black-and-tans' and betrayed my Irish blood. I was a traitor to my

family name and the enemy of a united Ireland. Vainly did I plead with him that my conversion concerned my soul: to him it concerned my nationality. He did not care if I was Methodist, Baptist or Presbyterian: by leaving Catholicism I was Protestant with all that that implied to him. Uselessly I attempted to draw attention away from politics to the cross: he refused to consider Christ a valid part of our discussion.

As for 'Rome', it really did not seem to notice my departure, and did not trouble to enquire after me. I was the subject of no inquisition and no denouncement. There were no Papal bulls issued against me, and no witch-hunts. The priest with whom I had discussed spiritual matters did not call on me. I don't think 'Rome' regarded my defection as a threat.

I think that people often expect me to say that leaving the Catholic Church was difficult, because of that denomination's claim to be the true Church of the Apostles, founded by Christ himself through Peter. The Catholic Church does claim, officially, that its Sacraments are our only effective means of salvation, and that without them we have no hope of heaven.

While I did not know Christ and him crucified, the above claims did hold me in thrall, but, as I have said before, I now have nothing to

fear. The Catholic Church, as an institution, does not frighten me, and I have no regrets about throwing in my lot with another religious group. I simply follow the One that feeds me, and I associate myself with those whom I recognise as his followers. If all my spiritual wants are supplied at other than my local Catholic Church, then other than my local Catholic Church is where I belong. No contest.

4

He Found Me - Gurnam Singh

What you are about to read is the story of how
God has changed the life of one man. If there
is any credit then it is God alone who will and
should receive it. There are some who believe
that he was deceived by Christians into changing his religion to follow Christ. Others have
said he was brainwashed. What follows will
hopefully clearly show that neither took place.
He prefers to regard his experience of being
drawn to Christ as a romance.

My Sikh upbringing

I was born and brought up in a Sikh home in
Nairobi, Kenya. Many Sikhs boast that their
religion presents a brotherhood with no other
caste system. Reality is very different! Our
family belonged to the tarkhans (carpenter), a
good, respectable caste. It originated in the
district of Jullandar in the Punjab, India.

Life at home centred on the Sikh religion. As
far back as I can remember both my parents
were extremely devout Sikhs as were my father's three brothers. They all had a very good

reputation in Kenya's strong Sikh community. My father and his brothers were partners in a carpentry business. Behind their workshop was a small room converted into a temple. It housed the Guru Granth Sahib, the religious book of the Sikhs. In between shifts and during breaks they took turns in reading through the Granth from cover to cover.

My father was well read having virtually educated himself in Kenya. He was able to secure a good job as a land surveyor with the Ministry of Works, after the business was sold. Over the years, he had read much about the deep things of the Faith. Astrology also became a keen interest with him. Many came from far and near to consult him about problems they were experiencing e.g. infertility, breakdown of marriages, inability to find a husband for their daughter, sickness, inability to produce male children etc. As he solved their problems via astrology he encouraged them to pray. He spoke to them a great deal about what he had read himself and taught various techniques of seeking God through Sikhism. I absorbed much of what he had to say to those desperate people and I believe it influenced me in my youth more than the other children in the family.

My mother was illiterate. In her youth it was not considered right for girls to go to school.

Educated girls posed a problem. She learnt Gurmukhi, the Panjabi script at home in India, by practicing to write it on the ground with her fingers. A ladies' meeting was held in our home every Thursday afternoon. A number of the faithful congregated together for a religious meeting. One of our rooms was dedicated to the Granth which was kept covered in colourful blankets on a raised platform.

You can well imagine the influence all this was to have on the youngest of seven children. Weekends and often evenings during the week were spent in the city temple. Occasionally, visiting religious groups arrived from India. They sang hymns from the Granth and retold the history of the Sikhs and their gurus to the gathered crowds. Many of their messages were recorded by us and played over and over again in our home. The whole atmosphere was permeated with the Sikh religion.

At the age of fourteen I was keen and ready for initiation into the Khalsa - the Sikh brotherhood. The ceremony is called Amrit-shakna and takes place in private in the presence of the Granth and the Khalsa as represented by five men. They are chosen because of their personal strict adherence to the vows being taken by the intending candidates. Some 'holy water' is drunk from a steel bowl and a little sprinkled

on the person being initiated. Vows are taken in the presence of the Granth and the Khalsa that one promises to wear the five symbols of Sikhism i.e. never to cut one's hair, wearing of a special comb in the hair, the carrying of a dagger, the wearing of a steel bangle and a special pair of shorts. In addition one takes vows to say prayers at least three times a day, the first to be said after having a wash before sunrise. Five sets of prayers from the Granth are repeated until one can know them by heart.

After going through my initiation ceremony my father taught me to read and write Gurmukhi, thus enabling me to read the Granth. Sometimes I led evening prayers for the family after which I ceremoniously prepared the Granth to rest for the night.

In 1980 I arrived in Britain as a young man, hoping to settle there after gaining a higher education. My brothers had arrived before me. By this time, my mother had passed away, so my father also came to Britain, in 1981. After taking my 'A' levels I enrolled at a polytechnic. After some time I was appointed Chairman of the Sikh Society. My task was to encourage the Sikh students in their faith. Most of them were nominal and were more concerned about promoting their culture than their religion.

First meeting with a Christian

It was then that I first met born-again Christians. The Christian union in the college had arranged a bookstall as part of an outreach Mission. One of course assumed that all Europeans were Christians. Contact with real Christianity was soon to persuade me of the falseness of this assumption. My attention was drawn to the bookstall. I was an avid reader of novels so was on the lookout for a bargain. The books on display were about Jesus Christ and the Christian Faith. I was noticed by one of the students on duty. He engaged me in conversation - what was to turn into a most enlightening and intriguing conversation. My first impressions of him were of his personal warmth and kindness. He put a number of questions to me.

Did I know anything about Jesus? I replied that I believed he died on the cross and rose again on the third day. I could remember films shown by a certain missionary in our courtyard in Kenya when I was a young lad.

Did I pray? I prayed a great deal since my search for God had grown over the years. I was becoming desperate. I practiced meditation as well (not in the Christian sense but in terms of repeating the name of God over and over again). The goal was to arrive at some sort of mystical experience where lights could be seen or sweet

music heard, or a combination of both. I was nowhere near achieving this. Here was someone who told me that when he prayed to Jesus he could speak to him directly. He could express to him all the desires of his heart. He knew that Jesus heard and answered his prayers. I had never heard anything like this was possible.

Did I know God? Everyone knows a little about him. He is Almighty, the Creator; some tell us he is omnipotent etc, but a personal knowledge of him is missing. This is what I was like as a Sikh. I was searching for him, trying to find him. I was doing my best but it was not enough. He was very far from me. I longed to be close to him. Again this man disturbed me by his experience of a personal knowledge of God.

Did I believe that I was a sinner? I knew that there were certain things in my life which were wrong. Yet I could not think of myself as a sinner having a sinful nature. I was a vegetarian who never ate beef or any other animal. I was taught that a Sikh was good, in fact better than the Brahmin, the highest caste of Hinduism. I was very proud that I was a Sikh.

Then came the crux of the matter. *What about assurance of salvation?* Did I know where I was going after death? Did my religion prepare me for heaven and give me a guarantee

that all was well with my soul? I answered that as a Sikh I believed in Karma. This law states that what you sow, you shall reap, some of it in this life and the remainder in the next. I aimed to do more good over and above all the evil that I might do in this life. At the end God would consider the balance and be pleased with what I did. I would be favoured with a better reincarnation. Release from the chain of reincarnation was as remote from me as the sun is from the earth. An assurance - none whatsoever!

My friend concluded that I must be a miserable man. His words were like an arrow to my heart. Something must be wrong somewhere. Nevertheless, I saw my chance of spreading the Sikh faith and expressed the desire to meet him again. He beamed in response. Through him I met many young people in the Christian Union. Their lives were different to those of other students. They seemed to have peace and contentment and an air of warmth and affection. It was clear that they loved God. I didn't even know him let alone love him.

Gradual appreciation of who Jesus is
I attended several meetings and heard many preachers speak about Christ. One I remember in particular. He spoke about the two sides of the cross and asked whether we were on the

saving side or the perishing. All depended on what one thought and understood about the meaning of the death of Jesus Christ. I believe that what I heard was used by God to convict me of sin, that is the reality of sin in my own life. Though what could be seen on the outside looked very nice yet, my own heart was deceitful and desperately wicked! I was in great need.

What I had considered wrong doing was really and truly sin against the Almighty and he was going to punish it with everlasting flames. I was carrying a heavy burden on my shoulders - the weight of my sins. I could feel myself sinking under it. Suddenly, my dead conscience had been awakened. In the light of hearing what God was like, the sin with which I trifled became very serious. It was the cause of separation between him and me. I heard much more and as I left the meeting I was trembling. I had much to think and reflect on.

As time went on I believe God overruled certain circumstances in our home, using them to bring me to my knees. This made me quite depressed and indeed desperate. Feeling very lonely and far from God I was brought to a crossroads. Which way should I turn? Should I become a Christian? Should I do this or that? I didn't know what to do. I didn't know who could help me even if I asked.

In the Bible, Jesus describes this experience,

No man can come to me except the Father which sent me draw him (John 6:44).

He was drawing me to himself and my resistance was beginning to break down. But, how could I leave everything that was so precious to me since my youth? How could I ever justify such action? Yet I did not have God, no life, no joy, no peace, no hope, no direction, no purpose, no heaven.

Just when I was at my most miserable a momentous event took place. It was to change the whole course of my life. I was invited to a church to hear a certain preacher. It was my very first visit to a church. I remember being impressed with the simplicity of the surroundings, and of the service. The preacher spoke from John 3:16:

For God so loved the world that he gave his only begotten Son that whosoever believeth on him should not perish but have everlasting life.

There are times when you hear and there are times when you 'hear'. I was 'hearing' that night. It was as if God was speaking to me, that night everything I heard was for me. I tell you that it was an experience out of this world.

Better than being in a space shuttle!

How ignorant I was about God and myself. Sin was destroying me and in that condition I was heading straight for hell. There was nothing I could do to change that. Only God was able by his grace. My sins had offended God and he was angry. I didn't even deserve any deliverance. If I did not believe, I would perish for ever and God would remain just in doing so. Yet, Jesus had done something for me which no other person had done. He died on the cross for my sins. He paid the penalty that I truly deserved. Why? Because of Love. Divine Love which has no beginning and knows no end. Also something undeniable. He was alive! He had risen from the dead! And twenty centuries later he still had power to save and forgive a sinner like me. He was alive; I could know him and speak to him; and he would come into my life. God, who was so far away, had come near to me in Jesus Christ. He would adopt me and become my Father in heaven. Praise the Lord!

Here it was, this is what I had been looking for all my life and I found it! I found God fully revealed in Jesus Christ and I was converted that day. I went home without the burden of all my sins. It was taken away from me and I was free. I was so full of joy that I had difficulty in sleeping for a few days.

Called to serve Jesus

I am grateful to the Lord for his faithfulness to me. Many trials were to follow: times of hardship and anxiety, yet the great difference was that he was with me. I was no longer alone, never to be forsaken by him. He remained my Rock and Hiding Place, the best shelter I could ever find.

Also I give thanks to God for the church. I came into the fellowship of God's people and we became members of one another in the body of Christ. People from the church were very kind and good to me. They supported me practically as my circumstances changed. I found support and love which will never be forgotten. Many prayed for me then and still do. May the Lord richly bless them.

Almost immediately, I sensed that the Lord was calling me into the ministry of the gospel. The fact that I was about to add insult to injury by studying for the Christian ministry, necessitated my having to leave home for my own safety. May I add that some months later I was happily reconciled with my family. My home church arranged for me to study at the European Missionary Fellowship's School of Evangelism, followed by training for the ministry at the London Theological Seminary. My heart's desire and prayer to God was that he would use

my life for his own glory in proclaiming the gospel to sinners.

After spending some time in two different Christian ministries in London, the Lord led me to Scotland. With hindsight I realise what excellent preparatory ground both situations were for the work in which I am now engaged. The church with which I worked in Southall had an interest in reaching Asian people with the gospel. This was a means of opening up to me the Lord's work among Asian people in the south of England. I have no doubt that my interest in reaching my own people from the sub-continent of India deepened during this time. My next calling was to a church planting situation in Paddington, London. Much experience was gained in relating to all types of people through regular door-to-door visitation.

It was in 1984 that I first came into contact with the Free Church of Scotland and their fairly new work amongst Asians in Glasgow. At that time Julia Mackenzie, who was later to become my wife, was the only missionary there. The following year, she was joined by a missionary couple, who had spent many years in India. After a period of further contact with this work, God began to so work in my life as to indicate that this was a door that he was opening up for me. Thus I arrived in Glasgow in September,

1988 to take up my new appointment.

The questions on the lips of many today are: "Why evangelise people who are already so religious? Are we not all worshipping the same God and eventually going to the same place?" I believe that those who reason thus know nothing of God's true revelation of himself in the Bible.

In Christianity, religion itself is transcended and left behind, all others being man-made ways of approaching God. The emphasis given is that man has to gain merit with God by his good works. This is in direct conflict with the gospel of the grace of God, where faith in the merits of Jesus Christ alone will give anyone a place in heaven.

I shall always be deeply grateful to God that there were people who took time to share the wonder of his love with me. Oh! for the joy of being used of God to bring other men and women to a knowledge of such a wonderful and precious Saviour.

He Found Me - Jeanette Fyfe

Make sure of all things (I Thess. 5:21). Ever since I was a child I have always thought this a very important statement for anyone claiming to have any knowledge of God and who seeks to pass that knowledge on to other people. So many people claim to know the truth and yet their basic beliefs are different. I was brought up as a Jehovah's Witness. I always believed I had the truth; as the years went by it became very clear that I was wrong.

My story begins in a mining area in South Wales. I was born in a town called Aberdare in Mid Glamorgan. My earliest recollections are of a big house next to a farmyard where I spent the first six or seven years of my life. I have two brothers and although there was never any parks or amenities close to hand, we did not mind because there always seemed to be acres of fields and a forest of trees to explore and make hide-outs in. We were sent to a Welsh-speaking school and, although we did not speak Welsh at home, somehow we learned the language and spoke it fluently. It has always been

a regret of mine that the language was forgotten when I moved up to an English-speaking school.

Brought up a Jehovah's Witness

It was during my childhood that I had my first introduction to religion through the teachings of the Jehovah's Witnesses. My mother had joined them when I was just a few months old and my father soon followed. I was taken every week to the meetings in the Kingdom Hall and I suppose I really enjoyed them. The people were always very happy and friendly and we settled quite naturally into their way of life. There were no creches at these meetings and we sat for up to two hours three times a week to listen to their Bible being explained to us, soaking it all up, even at a very young age. Children learn more than we often give them credit for. Even at the age of seven or eight, I knew what I believed and was sure I was right. I did not know why, but that was to come later.

I remember about this time, it must have been in the middle to late 'sixties', that we had a Christmas tree in the Kingdom Hall. Shortly after this, the Watchtower printed an article saying this was completely wrong and it was removed. You will not see one in the Kingdom Halls today. After we moved up from the Junior School it began to sink in just how differ-

ent and unpopular Jehovah's Witnesses were. We started to get a lot of criticism.

At this time I never questioned whether it might be us who were wrong, we just assumed that we were right. After all, children instinctively accept their parents' views because they trust them and looking back, my parents obviously believed the Witnesses and only sought to lead us in the way they felt was right. I was very happy with the Witnesses at this time and it wasn't until much later that I began to question their teachings, though I had started to feel isolated from everyone else at school and we knew we would never be allowed to join in various activities. Christmas, Easter, even birthdays were banned. The only event that was celebrated was a wedding anniversary.

Once a year we held the equivalent of the Lord's Supper, except that only one or two of the congregation were allowed to take the bread and wine because the rest were not part of the 144,000 chosen to reign with Christ in heaven. They would remain on earth and continue in God's ways but would not be part of the body of Christ - so could not share in the Lord's Supper. They were only the 'other sheep' (John10:16) or the 'Great Crowd' (Rev.7:9).

We did feel very left out of things at school but we were told that since we were doing right

God would bless us. It was quite difficult though when asked every year, "What did you get for Christmas?" to have to say we got nothing because we did not celebrate it.

My father worked in a smokeless fuel plant in South Wales and one of the saddest times of my life was when he took ill. He had been working so many extra hours and had become exhausted. When his mother died of pneumonia it was more than he could cope with. What followed was a long spell of depression from which he never recovered. We were still quite young and did not understand what was going on but things had changed in the house and it was not the happy place it was, only months before. It was no one's fault, it just happened.

He stopped going to the meetings at one point which worried us tremendously but my mother assured us that God understood how he felt and knew my father was doing his best. She was a great comfort at this time and looking back, I really don't know how she coped for so long with a sick husband and three growing children! I don't suppose that we were a lot of help to her at that time. We were growing up and had our minds on other things. Life plodded on at a fairly steady pace. My father was still ill but we coped with it. Then came the move to the Grammar School.

Up to this point, my brothers and I had always been together, but now I was on my own in an all-girl's school. I was very keen to get on with my studies but with growing up came the inevitable questioning. I had seen my father go downhill fast and I wondered whether all the hard work and effort would actually get me anywhere. We were discouraged from going to College or University because our main aim was always to work for God by going from door-to-door trying to get as many people as possible to join the Witnesses. I had decided that I would leave school as soon as I was sixteen and get a job to help the family, then spend the rest of my time going around doors.

I now regret that I did not stay on in school to get any qualifications. I am making up for that now, but then I only wanted to leave as quickly as I could. I did spend a lot of time knocking on doors. One summer holiday, I spent nearly a whole fortnight trying to get people interested in us. I was really proud of myself. It is hard for a teenager to keep up that kind of enthusiasm about God's work when all your friends are out doing other things; I did feel that I was missing out on life.

However at the age of fifteen, I was baptised as a Jehovah's Witness and really 'took off' in my interest in God. I also began for the first

time to ask myself why did I believe these things. Before I had always accepted the Witnesses' teachings since I naturally trusted them. Now I was starting to think for myself. There was a lot going on at the time. The Watchtower had predicted that the world was going to end in 1975 (a year after my baptism) and we were trying very hard to warn people in time. They all thought it was a big joke!

Disillusionment with the Jehovah's Witnesses

The only people that I had any reasonable conversations with were two girls at school who belonged to something called a 'Christian Union'. I wondered how anyone could possibly call themselves Christian and go to church. The Witnesses firmly believe that the Church is the Devil's greatest masterpiece. I was determined to prove them wrong! I even asked the elders' advice but their answers were never very convincing, even to me.

1975 came and 1975 went and with it my trust in the Watchtower Society. The world was still here and their 'prophecies' had failed again. I knew they had got the dates wrong on at least two other occasions and it had happened again.

'Miscalculation,' they said. I wondered how many miscalculations were acceptable for a

people who claimed to be God's voice on earth. The Bible tells us that the test of a prophet is whether or not what he says comes to pass. Was this the 'prophet' we were to follow? If the Jehovah's Witnesses had been so wrong, not just *once*, but *three* times, what else were they wrong about?

It was at this point that I prayed my first, sincere prayer. As I did not know who to trust, I went down on my knees and asked God himself to show me what was the truth. I had no other way of knowing. It was not very easy, a bit like trying to see what the weather is like without being allowed to open the curtains! All I had to go by was what the Watchtower Society told me. It all seemed very biased.

The elders refused to let me go to church with the girls to see what was taught for fear they would lose me to the Devil! Yet day by day, we asked people from all religions to come and listen to us. Was I just to accept their words blindly? My confidence in the Witnesses was already very shaky, and I could not accept what they said 'just because it's the truth' as one elder told me. How did I know it was the truth? I had no other standard to set it beside.

I never did find any reasonable answers to my questions from the Jehovah's Witnesses, even though I did go back a few times to see if

I really had made a big mistake. I honestly tried to give them the benefit of the doubt, but they could come up with no reasonable solutions to my questions about God.

I was disfellowshipped as a result of leaving home with a married man, which I am in no way proud of, but I think, in retrospect, that I was simply grateful to find a way out. I know it hurt my family a great deal, but I could not stay and commit myself to the Witnesses' teachings. I was totally confused as far as God was concerned. I suppose I was quite bitter too, I did not feel there was anyone I could trust and I just wanted to get away and be alone for a while. I did not see then how God was looking after me and leading me to the truth I so desperately wanted to find. I missed my family dreadfully, but did not feel I could go back: they had their own problems to contend with. It didn't take very long to hit rock-bottom; no job, no clothes, no money and no place to live.

Meets The Son of God

One day I was sitting on a wall beside the sea. I cannot remember if I actually prayed, but my heart was quietly hoping that God would do something! A young woman came up to me and asked me, "Do you know Jesus loves you?" I replied that of course I knew God loved me, I

was a Jehovah's Witness! I had been disfellow-shipped, but I was not going to tell her that. Again, she told me that Jesus loved me.

I knew about Jesus, but had never heard him spoken about in this way before. Although I had always seen him as God's Son, God himself had been the important one! There followed a lengthy conversation about the Church, the end times and the doctrine of the Trinity. I was well taught in the arguments against these things, but I still could not convince her, and she could not convince me! She asked me what I needed most of all, adding whatever it was, Jesus could provide me with it right then.

I was a bit taken aback. I had not heard anyone before who seemed to know Jesus as if he was her best friend! "Then tell him to find somewhere for me to live," I said, never for one minute thinking she would! I found myself spending the next three weeks sharing a house with her and her friends. They turned out to be a group of young people from *Youth With a Mission*, staying in the house while on a Summer Mission.

The other activity that struck me about them, apart from their kindness in picking up a total stranger off the street and feeding and clothing her, was the fact that they prayed so much! I am not talking about just rattling off words! Jesus

was obviously very special to them and they seemed to trust him in absolutely every decision they had to make. It wasn't a case of, "Lord, bless us today, for Jesus sake, Amen." It was real, heartfelt prayer, a pleading with God accompanied by a faith in him that I had never before encountered.

I didn't really have any intention of joining them, my early teaching in the Witnesses made me very wary. To begin with I did not know if I could trust them, yet day by day it became clearer that they knew what they were talking about. They showed me over and over again from the Scriptures that I could actually be saved *now*, a teaching that the Jehovah's Witnesses had always denied. But I could see it was true. All of Scripture backed it up.

I began to realise that I could never win God's favour by the number of hours spent knocking on doors, or trying my best. This was still not good enough to make me right with God. I had sinned repeatedly, and the penalty of sin was death. It was explained to me that Christ's death not only paid for my sin, but because he lives again, I could know his presence with me always and have his daily help in living as he wanted me to. God's demands are very high, but his provision in Christ meets them all. He would not only give me the

forgiveness necessary to come into his presence, but also the Holy Spirit to enable me to overcome wrong-doing. I could not lose this life within me, it would be there for ever.

For the first time, I saw it. God was not asking me to prove myself to him, but I could see that unless God himself changed me I never would.

I saw that I had been so wrong, and I thanked God for all that he had done for me. I knew I was right with him, because Jesus had made me right with him. I began to know what it felt like to have God as my best friend.

He Found Me - Malcolm Maclean

Christians, when they look back on their lives, often see great significance in many events in which they've been involved, and particularly in those over which they had no control. They were not involved in choosing their parents or deciding where their childhood should be spent yet that affects the rest of their lives. I can look back and trace the Lord's hand in guiding my life long before I came to know him personally.

Religious upbringing

I was born in Inverness, Scotland into a religious family. My parents and grandparents belonged to the Free Presbyterian Church of Scotland and my upbringing was based on the biblical teachings that were well-known and practised in that denomination. Very early in life, I was taught about my need of trusting in Christ to save me and of the necessity of having my sins forgiven. I went to Sunday School when I was five and during the following ten years, I learned many biblical passages as well as the entire Shorter Catechism and in the latter years

was given a good grounding in the Westminster Confession of Faith by the pastor in Inverness, the Rev. A.F. Mackay. I learned these lessons well because I had an excellent memory and today I thank God for the thorough instruction I was given then although I did not appreciate it for many years.

Several times during my childhood God spoke to me about my need of salvation. I can remember crying myself to sleep on one occasion, as well as at other times shaking with fear as I listened to preachers describing hell and eternal punishment. But as I grew older I began to doubt it all and by the time I was sixteen I did not believe any of it. I was still in school and living at home so I was expected to go to church. But during the church services my mind would be either at the football match I had attended the previous day or else anticipating the following week's activities. This period of my life does intrigue me and I don't know whether there is any connection between the fact that my interest in school receded when my interest in church died. Perhaps I associated them both with authority which I was beginning to dislike intensely.

The swinging sixties

During the mid 1960's I was strongly influenced by the culture of the period. The songs of Bob

Dylan, the dress and practices of the swinging sixties affected me greatly. I can remember the first time I saw Pink Floyd playing on television and I became an ardent follower of that type of rock music. My friends, whom I had met in secondary school, shared my general outlook on life. We despised all the teachings of the Bible, and lived lives that reflected that we only wanted to do what we felt like doing.

Relations at home were not good. I rebelled completely against the standards of my parents and it reflects their affection for me that they showed great tolerance with my manner of living. I am quite sure that most parents would have thrown me out of the home but they did not. As soon as I left school, I stopped going to church. Indeed I went out of my way to annoy those who attended it. I used to walk past the church building on a Sunday morning reading one of the Sunday newspapers; and sometimes on a Sunday evening, I would stand at the pub door at the time of the evening service so that passing church-goers who knew me would realize what I was doing. Yet I still remember that when I first entered a pub on a Sunday, I expected the roof to collapse on top of me.

I was now intent on enjoying life to the full and flung myself eagerly into as much activity as I could. The culture stressed 'do your own

thing' and I was determined to do mine. I dabbled in most of the activities that I thought would help me find myself. It was the time of flower-power and of listening to Eastern religions. The religious side of the latter did not appeal to me as I had come to the conclusion that all religions were basically a waste of time. But the idea of 'loving one another' was very interesting. 'Make love not war' was virtually the slogan of the period and I endorsed that heartily.

The idea of working to provide my needs did not attract me at all. From the time I left school until shortly after I was converted, I did not work regularly. Occasionally I would do a week's work if I needed money but my regular source of income was gambling in pubs. I don't think there was ever a time I had no money during these three years. Sometimes the state gave me financial assistance but the idea of having to apply and be interviewed did not interest me so usually I did not bother.

My friends began to dabble with drugs, mainly cannabis and LSD. I also tried them but did not develop any addiction to either although I did suffer the side affects, for about a year, of a bad trip I had with LSD. Several of my companions landed in trouble with the law over drugs with some being imprisoned. But today I am thank-

ful to God that I was kept from becoming addicted to drugs.

It was alcohol that was my main indulgence. I usually spent most of the opening hours in one of the local pubs. As well as enjoying drinking, I appreciated the company of fellow-consumers. It could be said that the pub became the main interest of my life as I played both darts and dominoes weekly for one of the local hotels. Occasionally I drank too much but normally I kept myself from being drunk.

Yet I was becoming disillusioned with such a meaningless existence. Was there not more to life than daily doing nothing except indulge in self-centred pleasure? I began to look to other areas to find meaning and satisfaction. One subject I began to think about was religion. I did not bother with Christianity because I thought I had tried it in childhood and was not interested in it any more. But I looked at others. I read most religious books in the public library, especially those describing various Eastern Religions. But I found them obscure and vague. I wanted something definite and reliable but I did not know where to find it.

Contact with Christians

Around this time, I discovered that local Christians were holding open-air services at the

Town Hall in Inverness. They were different from any other church-goers I had met. They were so happy belonging to Jesus that they wanted others to know him as well. This was something new to me. Before I thought Christianity was something so personal that you told nobody else. These believers were so content and full of the certainty of knowing Christ that they annoyed me. Probably this was because I had no certainty in my own mind about anything. I used to argue with them about the Bible. My upbringing had provided me with a good grasp of the Bible's teaching and often the situation was that I knew more about the Bible than did the young believer I was confronting. Yet I could not account for the joy he had and I was very conscious that they all had something I did not have.

Looking back to that period, I can see that the Lord was beginning to work in my heart. I was becoming more aware of the pointlessness of many things and was searching for what was real. I had not yet realised that the root of the problem was my sinful heart and mind. Yet several incidents that I can remember show how the Lord was ordering providences to affect me.

Suddenly I was barred from my favourite pub. I was falsely accused of something with the

result I could no longer go to it. This might not seem very important but it meant that I had to wait close by it for my friends to join me each Saturday night to go dancing or to a party. The most comfortable place was the seats at the Town Hall about seventy yards away. It was there that the Christians held their open-air. So I found myself each Saturday night for about a year discussing Jesus Christ with them.

Then another group of Christians came to spend a summer witnessing in Inverness. Somehow I ended up in one of their meetings. They insisted on giving a New Testament to me. I don't know why I took it since there were many Bibles at home. One night I was lying on my bed feeling depressed with life. I saw the New Testament and decided to read it. The portion that I read included the statement by Jesus, *I am come that they might have life and have it more abundantly* (John 10:10). This verse really shook me. Jesus, whom I thought had died two thousand years ago, was claiming to be the source of abundant life. I did not know what he meant but I began to think that my previous conceptions of him might be wrong.

About that time two of my acquaintances were killed in a road accident. I knew what the Bible taught about heaven and hell and began to wonder whether it was true. And if it was,

where were these people who had died? It was during this period that an incident took place that surprised but also challenged me. I was walking across a suspension bridge in Inverness when I saw a believer in my parents' church coming towards me. I was six foot two inches and about seventeen stone while she was about four and a half feet tall and thin. Most people of that church that I met either crossed the road when they saw me or else said something quickly as they rushed past. I was interested to see how she would react. She did not let her Lord and Master down because she spoke to me in a solemn yet loving way of the danger of me going to hell if I should die. I sort of laughed at her but really was quite impressed by her witness.

Another incident that I remember affecting me was this. I was outside the Town Hall with a friend. It was a wet night and we were sheltering in the doorway at about three in the morning. We saw one of the Christians who ran the open-air pass in his car. His name is Frank Peacock and both he and his wife, Caroline were to be a great help to me after I was converted. One of us commented that he would never come to speak to us on such a wet night. Yet he did. I do not remember anything he said. But I know that was the night I was convinced that Christianity was real in that Frank showed

his concern for me was consistent in all weathers. I began to search for God more earnestly.

The Lord began to show me that the problem was *me*. I was what the Bible called a sinner. Not only that but I was blind as far as seeing how I could get in touch with Jesus. I remember discussing it on several occasions with members of the Brethren Church who were holding the open-airs, but although I could in a sense appreciate the gospel intellectually, I did not understand what believing in Jesus meant. A Christian, who often witnessed to me, gave me a copy of Bunyan's autobiography, *Grace Abounding to the Chief of Sinners*, as he thought it would help me. I can still remember sitting up all night and reading it. But it was not until I was reading in one of C.H. Spurgeon's sermons that I grasped that I had to trust Jesus, and commit myself to him. I still remember how amazed I was at the simplicity of the way of salvation. It was trusting in Jesus and what he did.

Life as a Christian

I was now in another world or so it seemed. Verses in the Bible that I had learned in Sunday School came into my mind with meaning. There was great joy amongst my Christian friends from the open-air and I now joined them in their activities.

I still had difficulties. One was walking past a pub near my home. I had been in the habit of going there for a pint and now each time I passed it, I had a strong urge to enter. The only way I found to overcome this was to take detours to avoid passing it until the temptation stopped.

I also developed problems with assurance. With this the Rev. A.F. Mackay helped me. I contacted him with this difficulty over assurance and he came to my home to discuss it with me. He showed me the way out of my problem, and insisted on buying me a copy of *The Christian's Great Interest* by William Guthrie which helped to relieve me of my worries.

I was able to find work in a warehouse in Inverness although I had no references or anything to explain what I had been doing for the previous three years. The Lord also enabled me to cease smoking. I was smoking about forty cigarettes a day but soon after my conversion I was convicted about the sinfulness of this habit. With the Lord's help I stopped. I believe the reason some Christian's continue smoking and are not helped by God to give it up is because they don't believe it is a sin in so abusing the body God gave them.

During the years I have been a Christian, I have had three different jobs. For six years I

worked for a newspaper distributor as a ware-
houseman and van driver. I started work at four
thirty each morning Monday to Saturday. During the period that I worked there, the outlook
and quality of many of the newspapers deteriorated as far as Christian influence was concerned although in other areas improvements
were made. It finally reached the stage where
my conscience became very uneasy about being
involved in distributing them. So I decided to
leave.

I still enjoyed driving. Therefore, I went to a
HGV training school for a fortnight and passed
the driving test for a class one licence. I left the
work, and after two temporary driving jobs, was
employed by a national haulage firm where I
was to work for about ten years. For the first
four years I worked night shift driving from
Inverness to Perth or Alloa and the remaining
years on day-shift.

I greatly profited from my time there, and
not just in a financial sense. The long drives
between Inverness and my destination gave me
time to meditate, to pray and to listen to ministry cassette tapes. I enjoyed listening to tapes
by Christian teachers such as Donald Macleod,
Al Martin and John Stott. Also the stops at
loading points could last three to four hours
and I used these opportunities for preparing for

Bible studies and reading Christian books.

I can look back to the years I spent driving and thank God for the many things I learned during that period. One thing perplexed me though. During these ten years, I probably met hundreds of different people in connection with my work and only one was a believer. I have never met another Christian lorry driver.

In 1989 I was married and realized that log distance lorry-driving was not suitable for married life. It had involved long hours away from home and I did not believe it would help my marriage to grow if that continued. I did transfer to another branch which meant it was only local work in Inverness I was doing. But I began to want a change.

Then I saw an advert in a church magazine by a Christian organisation looking for a full-time worker. I applied for the position and after an interview, was offered the post and I gladly accepted. It is a totally new area for me but I find the work both challenging and satisfying. There has been a kind of culture shock however since I am now working in pleasant surroundings with committed Christians which is vastly different from being in the company of lorry drivers and mechanics.

My church commitment has involved three denominations. For about ten years I was a

member of a Brethren Church in Inverness. These believers were of great benefit to me. It was there I saw love in action for the first time as far as Christians were concerned. Each member who has helped me I value highly and I cannot express how much I owe them. Some of them are now at home with the Lord whom they loved and served while others are still good friends. Several of them were at my wedding and I counted that an honour for me.

However, I left the Brethren and rejoined my family in the Free Presbyterian Church. I had over the years become convinced that Calvinism is what the Bible teaches so I felt I should join a church that held to it. I was with them for about seven years and had not thought of leaving until a church dispute arose. While there I benefited from many of their activities. The communion seasons, a weekend of services associated with the Lord's Supper, I greatly enjoyed. The regular services that I heard instructed me and as I met with believers who loved the Lord, I counted myself privileged. It also helped as far as my family were concerned to be together in worshipping God. Since the dispute I have been in the Inverness congregation of the Associated Presbyterian Churches where we enjoy the Lord's blessing.

As well as being helped by various Chris-

tians, certain regular activities have helped me as a believer. I have been attending a Bible Study for about seventeen years. We have gone through most of the New Testament and parts of the Old Testament as well as a study on the Westminster Confession of Faith. These weekly studies have often been a spiritual oasis where we discovered wonderful things in God's book. Several members of the original study group are now serving the Lord full-time; two are ministers in the Associated Presbyterian Church and one is a Free Church of Scotland minister. It was also through the study group that I met the girl who was to become my wife. Katie was taken to it by a workmate. Our relationship developed until we were married about two and a half years after we met.

Another regular activity was a weekly gathering for prayer with several close friends. This prayer group lasted for seven years. Its purpose was to pray for our denomination in regard to its weekly services and also for friends who were in difficulty. Often these meetings were times of close fellowship with God as we simply told him about the burdens we felt. Although that group no longer meets, I now attend a monthly missionary prayer group which helps to keep me aware of the great need of vast numbers of people to hear the gospel.

The Christian life has its problems. We have spiritual enemies. Several times I have fallen but the Lord has graciously forgiven. The fact that I have reached this far is a testimony to the Lord's gracious care and blessing. Without him we can do nothing.

Whatever the past has been, the future is bright. Believers are travelling homeward but until they reach it, they can share the ambition of Paul who although writing from a prison cell thirty years after his conversion still aimed 'to know Christ' (Phil.3:10). The wonderful peace and joy that Jesus gives are stimulus for us to know him in deeper ways until the day when we shall see him face to face.

He Found Me - Elizabeth Rose

I was born in a castle, which sounds like a fairy tale. But none of us can choose what home and family we are born into. As the Bible says in Psalm 139, before we are born the Lord knows all about us and what will happen to us, and he even knows all our thoughts during the whole of our lives. He ordained marriage and family life for us although it is not everyone who has these things, but it makes all the difference if our homes, whatever they may be, are homely and are filled with love. Even castles can be homely and my mother did a great deal to make it so, although we were looked after by a nanny which, although she was a nice person, is not the same as being looked after by one's mother. I always found it difficult to converse with my parents as a result of this.

I was born on a Wednesday and my childhood and young adulthood were plagued by the rhyme in which 'Wednesday's child is full of woe'. I thought that everything was sure to go wrong because I was born on a Wednesday. When my sister was born two and a half years

later, she arrived on a Sunday and the rhyme said that, 'The child that is born on the Sabbath day is bonny and blithe and good and gay'. Everything seemed to go right for her; the adults preferred her because she always grinned and had golden curls while I had straight mousy hair. I was, however, very fond of my sister and enjoyed her company. I mention the rhymes because in my childhood I believed all the superstitions we were taught but, sadly, I did not believe the many children's hymns I learned and was not helped by them.

When I was ten my father arranged for a young man called Jimmy Duncan to hold a Children's Mission in the Castle. A few children from the town nearby came, along with four cousins living three miles away (I often played with them and shared a Governess with the two younger ones). My elder brother was away at boarding school so I was thrilled to have other children coming to the Castle in an informal way and not all dressed up, with their nannies in attendance. So my attention was focused on the children and I did not listen to what Jimmy Duncan was saying about Jesus.

Years later, when I had just come to know Jesus for myself, one of my flatmates started singing in the kitchen of our flat in London:

Wide, wide as the ocean,
High as the heaven above,
Deep, deep, as the deepest sea
Is my Saviour's love.

I said to her, "I know that song. Jimmy Duncan
taught it to us when I was ten." But I had not
taken in the meaning of it at the time or I would
have realised that Jesus loved me, however
unloved and lonely I felt.

Further impressions

I went to a day school when I was eleven which
I enjoyed very much. Two teachers there influenced me. One was the Art Teacher. One day
I drew a pony with plaits. She asked me who I
knew with plaits and when I said, "My sister,"
she said, " I think you are jealous of her." I was
although I still loved her very much.

The other influence was the Geography
Teacher when she taught my class about Australia. As I had some cousins who lived there I
decided that one of my ambitions would be to
go to Australia. God can guide through teachers. He certainly did guide me through these
two and I should like to thank them if I knew
where they were. I went to a boarding school
when I was thirteen as my parents had paid
insurance for our education there. My sister

and I did not enjoy boarding school. We missed the Castle and the friendliness of the little school.

When I was sixteen I was automatically confirmed into the Episcopal Church because my mother was English and wanted us to join the Episcopal Church although we had gone with my father to the village Church of Scotland until I was ten. Because I missed several classes through having measles I did not understand the idea of confirmation. I once asked a question, "What happens to all the people who are not confirmed?" but I did not receive an answer. I thought it was unfair that the fishermen in the town and all the other people who did not go to that school were not automatically confirmed. Why should I get an advantage which they were not getting? Years later I was given tickets to the Billy Graham Crusade at Haringay in 1954 and thought that my question was answered because the Crusade was fair and open to absolutely everybody.

I left school after one term in the sixth form. I hoped to get married and thought that art college would be interesting meantime. I did not think of a job as the only one suggested was teaching and I was much too shy to teach. It did not occur to me to pray about what I should do when I left school. I did not know that Jesus was really interested in every aspect of my life and

that he knew exactly what would suit me and be the best thing I could do.

My brother was killed in El Alamein while I was an art student. This was a terrible blow as he was a wonderful person and a marvellous brother. I did not know then that he had received Jesus Christ for himself when he was thirteen, at a Scripture Union Camp, and so was ready to die. But I was glad to have had such a lovely brother for so many years and I was quite sure he had gone to heaven which was a great consolation to me. We do well to appreciate people while we have their company and do everything we can do to help and encourage them while we have the opportunity.

At the College of Art I learned a lot about drawing and painting. But then, as the War still went on, I had to join up and went into the WRNS where I became an Engine Air Mechanic, the qualification for this being Elementary Maths. My sister got married just after VE day and I got leave to be her bridesmaid. After VJ day I was moved to Crail on the Fife coast where we, Wren Air Mechanics, sang in the choir at the Sunday services. I made four good friends during my time as a Wren. When they no longer required Wren Air Mechanics I became a Pay Writer. I found office life very cramping after the freedom of the Airfield and

thought I would never work in an office again. How wrong I was!

Emotional stress

Before the Pay Writers' course started I should have asked for leave to visit my old father (he was 83 and very poorly) but I did not do so. I regretted it bitterly afterwards as while I was on the course, 500 miles away my father died suddenly. I was reminded of this years later when a young secretary colleague, who was a Christian, told me she was going home 100 miles to see her Grandmother for the weekend. I did not know the Lord at this time and did not either hear or listen to him.

I was given compassionate leave to go home for my father's funeral. Suddenly I realised that as my brother had been killed I was now the heiress and had the responsibility of the Estate although my mother had the life rent of the Castle. During my leave, my sister gave birth to the first of four boys which she had before she was twenty-five.

Six months later my mother had a hernia operation and my aunt suggested that I ask for release on compassionate grounds to come home and look after my mother, which I did. After that I went down to London to be near my sister who lived in Surrey.

While there I went to another Art School where I was introduced to a girl whose landlady was going away, leaving her with a young lad boarder for whom she had to cook breakfast. She asked me to come and share her room and cook breakfast for him on alternate days. One day when I came in late I found her in bed with a Medical Student. I was extremely shocked and disgusted as this was not common then as it is now. I did not know what to do - the girl and I had arranged to stay in another flat together as soon as the landlady returned. I should have told her I was not going to share with her any longer but the situation seemed impossible to me at the time.

The Easter Holidays came soon after this and I decided to go home. Miraculously, the Lord had put one of my sister's brother's-in-law, whom I had known since childhood, on the same train. We had dinner on the train but I don't think I told him my troubles as I was very shy and silent in those days. I had a sleeper to myself but I could not sleep and felt quite desperate. I got up to jump out of the train. But a woman was standing in the corridor which made me stop. I then remembered that my family and friends would miss me if I did jump out. Almost everybody has someone who cares for them, and even if nobody appears to care

God does. I thank God a billion times over that he delivered me from this terrible brink of destruction.

When I arrived home I could not sleep and suffered a nervous breakdown. My mother and aunt drove me to a distant hospital because, in those days, it was a sort of disgrace to have a breakdown. On the way I noticed for the first time in my life the exquisite beauty of the countryside in Spring. I suddenly realised that God was the Creator of it all and that he was my Creator too. I thought in those days that since I was in hospital I was likely to die and how terrible it was that I had only just become aware of God and I had never done a thing for him. I did not realise at the time that no matter what I did for God I could not earn my way to heaven; and that it was in accepting Christ and his sacrifice for my sins on the cross that would make me ready to face God when I died; and that Christ could live within me and help me. I did not know this and felt lost.

My mother came to see me every day but did not know how to help me. But one day I was so thrilled when my sister came to see me with her third baby and put him in my lap; someone trusted me and did not think I was out of my mind. When we went for a walk together I said to her, "I will be out of this place within a

month." I was, praise the Lord. He can use various people to help us at different times.

After a Cookery Course I wanted to do something for other people, especially children and was able to get a job as Third Matron at a Preparatory School. I loved this and am still friendly with three of the staff I met there. But when they heard I had had a breakdown they said that I must leave at the end of the year. However it was all in God's hands. Owing to a teacher coming back for the last term, after being away for two years in Australia, I said to her, "I've always wanted to go to Australia." She said, "Well, why don't you go?"

Foreign trips

So I went to a Cargo Shipping line and booked my passage to Sydney where a cousin and his wife lived. The fare was £90 and I was away for eleven months. The Lord put me in a cabin with a lovely Christian girl of about my age and we had both brought sketchblocks, embroidery and knitting to do. I studied Portuguese as well, hoping to visit a friend in Lourenco Marques on the way back, which I did. The girl was very shy and did not speak to me of Christ. Later on I did stay at her home and went to her church and was amazed when her father who was not a minister was able to pray aloud. Apart from

staying at my cousins, I stayed in the YWCAs in all the big cities and even went up to Cairns and down to Tasmania.

I could not get a job, so came back on another Cargo Boat to Africa. I did have a fortnight in Lourenco Marques and a weekend in Johannesburg with my friends. I then flew to Cape Town instead of going by train as I had developed a grumbling appendix which had to be removed there. The Lord put me in a Nursing Home, run by Irish Nuns and Nurses. I was able to board the intended ship eight days after the operation. I was even allowed to swim on the boat.

A distant cousin in Melbourne had suggested I become a secretary like his daughters. I thought it would be useful to know how to deal with the business letters involved in running the Estate. So a friend booked me in at a Secretarial Course in London. I became a secretary and my first job was with an International Congress on old age. I also worked for solicitors in Grays Inn, for a Bureau on temporary work for some months and also as secretary to the Headmaster of a Preparatory School.

Six years after I visited Australia, my sister with her husband and four boys emigrated there. In 1962 I went to visit her. On the ship coming back I shared a cabin with another lovely

Christian girl who was a physiotherapist. When I returned, I got a job as a secretary to the Principal Tutor in the Nursing School of the Middlesex Hospital. After some months I moved into a flat with the girl who had been my cabin mate. I met the girls who had been in the flat previously as they kept coming and staying with us. I thought all these girls had something about them, an indefinable joy which I did not have.

Christian friends

I was continually frustrated and desperate because I had not got married. Yet all these girls were spinsters and I could not think why they were so happy. One of them took me to All Souls Church, Langham Place, to hear John Stott but I said I could not understand the sermon. She then asked, "Why don't you read his book, *Basic Christianity*?" I did, a chapter a night. In it he says that a lot of people think they are real Christians because they live in a Christian country or because they go to church. (I was by this time going to church three times on Sunday but I did not seem to know much about God, although I was trying to read the Bible with the Bible Reading Fellowship notes which I had got in a church near the Preparatory School.) I read on to see what did make one a

Christian and realised that I needed a personal relationship with Christ. I suddenly realised what was lacking in my life and asked Christ into my heart.

Although I sent a number of people copies of *Basic Christianity* I did not tell anyone about my conversion. A few weeks later I had a new flatmate and one night I invited a fellow secretary from the hospital to our evening meal. They recognised each other as Christians and began talking about their conversions. They asked me when I was converted, so I said about four weeks ago. It turned out that the secretary, with another secretary, had been praying for my conversion.

My flatmate, who was a teacher at All Souls Primary School, said that I should go to a Bible Class and that she would ask John Stott about it. I had never heard of a Bible Class in any of the churches I had been to and had thought they were only for ministers. But I went to a Bible Class at All Souls and the next year to a Commissioned Workers Class and became an Old People's Visitor.

My secretary friend took me to a conference of the Middlesex Hospital Christian Union. I did not want to go as the word 'Conference' sounded boring to me. While there I realised that the building had once been someone's

Victorian home and now was a conference centre in the winter and a holiday place in the summer. The Lord put it into my mind that it might be possible to turn my castle into a similar place, and my teacher flatmate and also a Christian solicitor thought so as well.

Use the castle for Christ

My mother was too old to face such a change but she came to two Christian Conferences with me. (It had been at a conference of the Officers' Christian Union that she and my father had been converted in 1927.) I visited Australia again in 1965. While there I attended the Central Coast Crusade in New South Wales which was held a mile from my sister's home. I joined the choir so that I could go every night and after the Crusade I was baptised as a believer.

I had to return earlier than planned as my mother had two strokes and was already unconscious when I arrived. She lived seven agonising weeks during which I could not believe she was dying. She died in April 1966 and by May 1967 we were able to open the castle as a Christian Guest House. The Lord opened up the way for us and we had the Rev. D.P. Thomson to dedicate it at an opening ceremony.

In the winter of 1967 I attended the Capernwray Bible School. I learned a lot about the

Bible and made some good friends with whom I still correspond and occasionally see. The Lord helped me overcome my intense fear of speaking in public as we had to take part in outreach at the weekends.

While I was at the Capernwray Bible School, one of the students who was from Mexico asked me if we had Youth Groups in the castle. I replied, "We have had a Free Church Youth Group but we are not really suited to Youth Groups." He said, "Have you any chalets or an old barn which you could use?" I said, "Yes, we have an old barn which we were going to modernise into two flats."

The Lord helped us in many ways and the local workmen went to work with a will so that the work was completed and the barn transformed the following year. I had a 'curtain factory' in my room and machined the curtains while some friends pinned them up, and others helped to put together the bunk beds. We were also able to have a Conference Hall, which holds 200, built near the Castle and it is always filled to capacity when the Brethren hold their annual Conference week.

We have people of all denominations and nationalities coming (even atheists), and some return year after year. Others just spend a night while they are passing through on a brief visit to

Scotland. We now try and give some Christian witness as we lead guided Historical Tours of the castle as there have been some keen Christians among my ancestors. Also at the end of breakfast and dinner while everyone is still sitting at the table the manager reads some verses of Scripture and gives a brief message.

How good is the God we adore. I was born in the castle for the first time, and a number of people have been 'born again' spiritually there in the way the Lord explains in John 3:3. I trust there will be many more people having their 'second birth' in this castle which has a homely, peaceful and joyful atmosphere and where 'Christ is the head of this house.'

He Found Me - Donald Macleod

My story* is very undramatic and very uninter-
esting. In fact I feel reluctant to draw any
attention to my own experience in any way
whatever. But that is what has been asked for,
and there is, of course, some warrant for it as
the New Testament itself shows. Paul, more
than once, recited his own experience of God's
grace and God's saving power; and so I mention
a few things of a personal kind this evening.

Christian home

I must say, first of all, that from my earliest
childhood I was surrounded by Christian people. I was brought up in a Christian home and
that home was always full of visitors who were,
for the most part, believing Christians. I am
profoundly thankful to God for that experience
because my early years are linked in my memory with many hours of what I can only call the
most edifying entertainment. Many of the men

*This is an address given in Urray Free Church in October,1987.
It is reproduced here very much as delivered. Hence the idiom
of the spoken, rather than the written, word.

who came to the house had been on active war service. They were, from every point of view, men's men: men of courage, men of experience and men of integrity. They were also men who were endlessly kind to children; men possessed of a keen sense of humour; men of enormous intelligence and wit; above all, men who loved to argue about and to discuss the truth of God. It was my privilege to sit, sometimes for hours, as these men (and women) described the way God had led them, and as they shared their views on the great topics of Christianity.

I remember the late Professor John Murray telling me that he once asked a little boy in a Free Church manse, "What do you like best about the Communions?" and the little boy replied without hesitation, "I like the trifles!" Now, I'm sure I had my share of that as well, but my memory is very much of the fellowship, of the camaraderie and of the excursions into the truth of God. These things made an impression which remains with me to this day. From my earliest years I wanted to make these people my people.

When I went to Glasgow to study, I searched for the church my parents had once attended, the Highland Free Church in Partick. I received a great welcome. The man who was at the door that Sunday will never know how much

it meant to me, fresh from the Islands, to meet somebody who was so interested, and so concerned to make me feel at home. Over the years since then it has been my privilege to meet many other Christians whose lives came to be bound up with my own. They were men of different strengths and aptitudes, some men of great intellect, some who combined intellect with evident piety and heavenliness of demeanour. Some are close friends who, in adversity, have shown invincible personal courage. Others could not read, yet could discuss the most recondite areas of God's truth in a way that, in my experience, few theologians could match.

But I have no doubt whatever that I owe my faith to the magnetism of those men and women who came to our home those many years ago. I find it is still the same: that in moments of personal anguish I am helped by the recollection of some whose paths have crossed my own and in whom, I remain confident, there was a power, a grace and a beauty that were not of this world. I do not want to mention names. But I do want to remind those who are leaders in the church of the enormous importance of personal contact. How much can hinge on the impression we make on casual visitors to our churches! Nothing can replace the impact of man upon man and woman upon woman.

Spiritual anguish

The second point I want to make is this: during my student years I went through a time of great spiritual anguish, something of which I have not said much in private and never in public until this evening. It was an experience of radical doubt, an experience in which I lost, or seemed to lose, all my faith in God. The questions were posed to me at a radical and personal level - Does God exist? Is the Bible God's Word? Is Jesus Christ really still alive and still the Lord of all?

I shall say just two things about that experience. First of all, it was not due to any particular argument. It was not that anybody came with any striking show of learning or logic to undermine my faith. It was not based on scholarship or study or exposure to any kind of organised scepticism. It was simply, as far as I understand it today, something that came directly from hell itself.

It was a question. It was the sowing of a seed of doubt and in a single moment all the lights in my world went out: no faith in God, no faith in the Bible, no faith in Christ.

The second point I would make is that it was a thoroughly miserable experience. I understand that there are atheists in this world who are happy; that there are men and women

under conviction of sin who sometimes wish that God didn't exist. But it was not that way with me. For me it was desolation. It was darkness. It was a world without hope, a world without joy, a world without meaning and a world without purpose.

It began in the year of Glasgow's last great smog. I suppose most of you have never known a Glasgow smog, but it means virtually impenetrable darkness, even during the day; and that in many ways matched my condition in that state of doubt. I do not want to dramatise it. I remember envying ministers because they had been called by God and that meant that they had met God and they knew that he existed. I envied them most fervently. They had seen the light. God had spoken to them. I remember one evening going to hear a certain preacher. I went because he was a Professor and a Doctor of Divinity, with endless letters after his name, and I thought, "This man will meet my need and convince me again that God exists." I went with a longing soul but the man told stories and I got nothing to meet my need.

I shall leave it there. The years passed: years during which I prayed; years during which I stuck with God's people. And I studied. I seemed to have the whole of Glasgow University's theological library to myself: thousands

and thousands of books in which I searched for
answers to the questions troubling my soul.
Theology was not then (as it may be now) something one does detatchedly and dispassionately.
It was something I did for survival because I had
to find answers. At last, after waiting and
waiting, studying and praying, God took me out
of that pit and placed my feet on the Rock.

The existence of God

That is the background. Why, then, am I now a
Christian? Let me take the existence of God
first of all. Why do I believe that God is? Let me
take you to Romans One. There Paul describes
man, the human race, as being surrounded by
revelation. To man, the things that are made,
the things that are visible, tell the glory of the
invisible God. They speak of God's eternal
power and Godhead. Paul says that the experience of every man is that that revelation of God
impinges upon his conscience, so that every
man knows that he is dependent upon God,
knows that he is answerable to God and knows
that he is under obligation to God. We know
the voice of conscience: the word 'ought'. Paul
tells us that every man is made in such a way that
he invariably infers from the world around him
the eternal power and Godhead of God. This
awareness of God is utterly ineradicable. It

never goes away. Even though we sink to the very abyss of depravity, that awareness is still there. We know the judgment of God (Romans 1:32). That is always with us. Inescapably and invariably we are conscious of God.

I went to John Calvin. I found him explaining Paul's teaching. I found Calvin saying to me that there is a sense of deity in every heart. I heard Calvin saying that God has sown the knowledge of himself in every heart. I heard Calvin saying that the seed of religion is in every heart. I heard Calvin saying that there is no man so brutalised but that his conscience, at least now and again, summons him before God's tribunal. And I knew that all Paul said, and all that Calvin said, was true of me. I know that even in those days when atheism seemed to be engulfing me, I prayed, I stayed with the people of God and with the Word of God because there was this sense of deity and this seed of religion, this inescapable awareness of God. All that was true of me.

I am not going to philosophise, but it is very interesting that we always assume that things have a meaning. All that happens in our lives, the various episodes and the problems we face - we always assume these things have a meaning. We assume that things matter. We ask for explanations. We get angry. We praise. We

blame. Now that is an amazing thing, because if God does not exist, if there is no ultimate Being, the whole big picture, the whole story, makes no sense. Then how can the wee bits make sense? Why do we ask 'why'? Why do we look for reasons, for explanations? Why do we praise people? Why do we blame people? Why do things matter? All the time we are assuming that things have a meaning. But that makes no sense at all unless, as I say, the cosmos has meaning. In other words, if the aggregate - the whole big thing - does not make sense, then how can the little bits make sense? And yet you and I have to live assuming unavoidably that things are always making sense.

I was particularly impressed, and still am, by the scientists, although to many Christians they are the bogeymen. And yet, you know, in many ways the scientists give me so much comfort because they, above everybody else, keep on assuming that everything has a meaning. They assume that this world has a logic, they talk about chemical bonds and they make projections and predictions and they prepare their graphs - they are doing it all the time because they assume that the whole world around them makes sense and has a purpose. The astronomers assume that the courses of the planets, the millions of galaxies, have a pattern. Physicists

assume that electrons perform according to a certain logic. They can even plot the margins of the indeterminate. The biologist assumes that genes and chromosomes have their own pattern. To me that faith in order is absolutely marvellous. And I know why the galaxies have a pattern. I know why genes and chromosomes have a pattern - because the world was made by the Word of God. The Word is *Logos*, the logic of God, and this world is Logical. The scientists assume that things have a pattern, but it can only be logical because it was made by the wisdom of God. It was made, as Pascal said, by a pure mathematician. You can take practically any physical feature in this universe and can describe it in a mathematical way.

The physicist, the biologist and the housewife are always assuming that things make sense. All our anger, all our marches and demonstrations, all our questions, all our praise and blame, point to this great fact: we have to assume that things make sense. For me, that means that we have to assume God.

The question is: If this world did not come from God, then where did it come from? For many decades now the Christian doctrine of creation has been under attack, and we have allowed ourselves to remain under attack. I want to counter-attack: If you take it away,

what do you put in its place? The biggest miracle of all is that this universe actually exists. No-one can deny that. But where does it come from? The problem is that the man in the street assumes that the scientist has disproved God. But what is the alternative? In my judgment there are only two other possibilities. It is possible, for example, that this world came from Nothing. I wonder if the youngest folk here tonight have ever tried to imagine *nothing*? Nothing is not the numeral 0 (zero). The numeral 0 is something, but nothing is nothing. Nothing is absolutely nothing. Now we are asked to believe that this world came from nothing; that before this universe there was absolutely nothing. If the world came from nothing, then this vast universe and everybody on it and all the achievements of the human race have all come from nothing. I find that quite incredible.

Or again, it is possible that this world came from an impersonal something: some lump of matter. We can call it, simply, 'The Lump'. This Lump is supposed to have created this whole universe: those sub-atomic particles with all their potencies; the human genes and chromosomes with all their precision; and all the achievements of the human spirit. Out of it - out of this Lump - there came Hamlet, there came

Michelangelo, there came the Gospel of John.
Out of it there came even Jesus Christ himself.
It has to be an eternal Lump and an omnipotent
Lump. It has to have inside it all the prog-
rammes and all the blueprints. What can I say?
If I could find this Lump, I would worship it.

There are the only three options. Either the
world came from nothing, or it came from the
Lump, or it came from God; and it certainly
seems to me much easier to believe that it came
from an eternal and infinite intelligence than to
assume that it came either out of Nothing or out
of some primitive, impersonal Something.

Is the Bible the Word of God?
Then I come to the question, Is the Bible the
Word of God? Why do I believe it is? As a
matter of simple history, I suppose, I believe it
because it was commended to me by the people
of God. And then it was commended to me by
the Apostles of Jesus Christ: *All Scripture,* says
Paul, *is given by inspiration of God* (2 Tim. 3:16).
Above all, it was commended to me by Jesus
Christ himself: *The Scripture*, he said, *cannot be
broken* (John 10:35). It was these three things
that sowed in my heart the belief that the Bible
is the Word of God: what Christians told me,
what the Apostle Paul told me, what Jesus
Christ told me. That faith, as I said, subse-

quently came under attack. Indeed, I have become very conversant with such attacks during the last thirty years or so. Yet I still believe that it is God's Word, inspired in its every utterance and infallible in all that it says and in all that it intends to teach us.

Why do I believe this? Why do I love and adore the Bible as the Word of God?

First of all, because the Bible describes me with incredible accuracy. It seems to me to paint me so vividly when it speaks of the depravity of man, of the duplicity of man, of all the imaginations and thoughts which are only evil continually. I understand that there are some who very much resent that teaching. But I don't resent it for a single moment. It describes me with perfect accuracy. I cannot by myself see the Kingdom of God. In myself I hate God. In myself I am selfish. My temperament is difficult to manage. I find great teaching in God's Word about anxiety, about discontent, about depression, about paranoia; and it has never told me a lie about myself. I find that it describes me, that it understands me so very well; there is not a single statement in the Bible about men, about the human race, about Christians with which I would quarrel, because I know that all its judgments and its pronouncements are true of myself.

Secondly, I find in this Bible the proclamation of a matchless remedy. As well as finding the description of my own sin, I find a matchless remedy. Samuel Davies speaks of God in these terms:

> Great God of wonders, all thy ways
> Are matchless, Godlike and divine.

The way the Bible describes God and God's salvation to me is exactly and precisely that. It is matchless, Godlike and divine. It meets my highest expectations. I could not imagine a greater salvation than the salvation that has been secured by the incarnation, by the enfleshment of God. I cannot imagine anything more moving or more eloquent of God's love and God's concern than that God should give his Son for my salvation and that this Son should in my nature hang on the cross of Calvary bearing what my sin deserved. That to me is matchless, Godlike and divine. And I cannot imagine anything more splendid in terms of divine provision to help me along the Christian way, than the great promise and great reality of the indwelling of the Spirit of God. I am saying the remedy is matchless. The incarnation is matchless. The atonement is matchless. The indwelling of the Spirit is matchless. These things are the great central message of the Bible and they

are the marks of the Bible's own divinity, its own heavenly origin. The Bible speaks in a way that is matchless, Godlike and divine.

Thirdly, I believe the Bible because for thirty years now I have tested it and tested it and tested it. It has been my privilege to be called to preach the gospel - and that *is* a privilege - and if there have been days when I wanted to quit, it was not because I was tired of the work but because I was convinced that I was ill-equipped for it and undeserving of it. But in pursuit of that calling I have had to look at the Bible - especially at the New Testament - with microscopic intensity. I have looked at the plans of the books, and at questions of authorship, purpose and origin. I have looked minutely at particular verses. I have looked at the word-endings, at the tenses and the genders and the cases. I have looked at the question of punctuation - where should the commas go? - and at the question-marks, because we do not have these in the original. I have looked at the textual variants. And not only have I done it, of course, but all my colleagues at the College have done it; and millions of others have done it.

I can say, as all preachers of the gospel can say, that it is the greatest thrill in life to sit down with a verse from the Gospel of John or the Epistle to the Romans and look at it closely: the

beauty of it! the grandeur of it! the surprise! So very, very often I have gone to a verse with some pre-conception of its meaning and it has come to me with a completely different message, more profound, more glorious, more moving. I am not sure, but I sometimes think that the greatest single argument for the existence of God is the Gospel of John. Whoever wrote that Gospel, whoever is behind it, I would worship him. There is something there that is unparalleled anywhere else. John's use of little, little words to build up great massive truths. The greatest sentence ever penned consists entirely of tiny, little words:

> In the beginning was the Word and the Word was with God and the Word was God (John 1:1).

Wee, tiny words. Little words. You take them and put them under the microscope and they are matchless, Godlike and divine. We ought to be literally driven from our chairs as we study this Word and see something of what it says. Looking at its accents, its syntax, its grammar, we have to ask, "What is God saying to me? Why is it aorist and not present? Or why is it perfect and not aorist? And so on."

All this incredible complexity of grammar in this great work! If my faith ever flags - and I thank God it does not do so much nowadays -

the remedy is to go back to the Bible and there come face to face with the mind of God. To me, this Bible is itself a great object of wonder; an outcropping of God; a proof that he is there. Here, someone speaks who knows me. Here, someone offers me something that is quite matchless; and here somebody uses words in a way that is absolutely peerless. In that Greek grammar there is so much of the living God!

Is Jesus Lord?

The third question is this: Why do I believe that Jesus Christ is Lord? Why is my life controlled by him? Why do I bow the knee to him?

I want to begin here with two witnesses. I want to go back first of all to the Apostles, and especially to two of them because they meant so much to myself in my own struggles. There was the Apostle Paul. He was the man who of all men in the world was the least likely to become a Christian. He was a fanatical Jew. He was a bigot. He was self-assured. He was moving rapidly to the climax of a marvellous career. And he absolutely loathed and hated Jesus Christ.

People ask sometimes, 'Did Paul mean it when he said that he was the chief of sinners? Was it only the language of someone under conviction of sin?' Don't think it for a moment!

Saul of Tarsus was the greatest danger the Church of Christ ever faced. In fact, he came very, very close to strangling that Church in its cradle. But one day, on the road to Damascus something happened that unbelieving scholars have never been able to explain.

An American scholar, J. Gresham Machen, to whom I personally owe an immense debt, wrote a great book some sixty years ago called *The Origin of Paul's Religion*. That book asked one simple question: 'What made Paul a Christian?' There is only one answer, the answer Paul himself gives: *It pleased God to reveal his Son in me* (Gal.1:16). Paul was absolutely convinced that on the Damascus Road he had met the living Christ. All his prejudices disappeared in a moment. He became so sure that Christ was Lord that he spent the rest of his life preaching him; and eventually laid down his life for him. That is why the Damascus Road is one of the greatest moments in history. So much depended upon it! In fact, you and I would not be here tonight were it not for the eruption of God into the life of Saul of Tarsus at that time and at that place.

And then I think of the Apostle James. James is very special because he was the Lord's brother. They had lived in the same home. They had, outwardly, the same father and mother. They

had eaten at the same table. I suppose they had even slept in the same bed. And James was a Jew of the Jews. He was known in Jerusalem as James the Righteous. Even those Jews who loathed the Christians could find no fault with him. The incredible thing is that although he slept in the same house as Jesus he began his epistle with the astonishing words, *James, a slave of God, and of Jesus!* (James1:1). That surely is a remarkable testimony. A member of the same family and yet he calls him his Lord! A Jew, and he calls his brother Jehovah!

There are two things which constantly weigh with me as I reflect upon Jesus Christ.

The first is this. I do not believe that anyone could have created Jesus Christ. I am told by many scholars today that he is a creation of the Gospel writers. I find that utterly incredible. This Man who criticises the Apostles, criticises his own culture, who moves so freely among women, who teaches the most splendid parables, who preached the Sermon on the Mount, who prayed the prayer of John Seventeen - who created him? Which of the Gospel writers had the literary genius? They were unlearned men, unlettered men - which of them created Jesus?

Then there is this that weighs with me: that he is unsurpassable. Anselm once said that 'God is that than which a greater cannot be

conceived'. To me Jesus Christ is exactly that: a greater cannot be conceived. He is great in the glory of his person, as the God-man, that marvellous combination of transcendence and elevation on the one hand and compassion and sympathy on the other. He is great in his teaching, great in his work and great in his promises. Where would I improve him? Where would I alter him? Where is his equal? Where is his superior?

If I couldn't worship Jesus Christ I would worship the man who created him. I remember constantly the great words of William Guthrie of Fenwick: when faith looks at Christ it says, 'Less would not satisfy and more is not desired.' For me the search for truth ends with Christ. Less would not satisfy me; more is not desired. If this light went out all the lights would go out.

Many of you have never known my kind of struggle. I am not sure that I envy you. But I do marvel at many of you. It seemed to me, it seems to me still, impossible to believe that Jesus is Lord without bowing the knee. And yet many people in our churches do just that. How I envied all those adherents who had no doubts! How I wondered that their knees were not bowed! The moment I saw the truth I had to bow the knee.

9

He Found Me - Margo Macaskill

I was born on the 19th February 1943, in a
family of nine. Being brought up in a Christian
home I was introduced to the gospel story from
childhood, but sadly it was not until I was 35
years old that I knew Christ personally.

Growing up in a Christian family

We lived in the country and I have many happy
memories of childhood spent playing in the
wooded areas among the heather and bracken.
It was wonderful for imaginative games, and
there was no shortage of these. All of this
carefree, untroubled childhood was surrounded
by loving parents whose main aim was to see all
their children come to know Christ. Naughti-
ness was punished and there being nine of us,
my father and mother, no doubt, were sad on
many occasions. We got up to many pranks and
our home seemed to be always invaded by other
children. Children attract children and I suppose that is what happened with our home.

Many are the memories of my father gathering us all around and teaching us Bible Truths,

praying with and for us. My father on occasions would call us in from our play and send us all to our bedrooms to pray, such was his concern for us. Although Christ and his work was explained to me time and time again, I felt no real need or desire to know Christ personally. In fact I disliked the very idea.

One night while lying in bed with my younger sister we were talking about things that we would most like to have. I had seen a doll that I would have loved - if only I could get it. My sister said, "I'd just love to get a ladder and climb right into heaven to be with Jesus." I thought it a crazy idea and felt it was the last thing I wanted. Another time I remember one of our teachers in Primary School telling us about the crucifixion. I noticed my sister was crying and when I asked her why she was crying she said that she was sad that they did such cruel things to Jesus. I was totally unmoved.

Church and Sunday School were very much a part of my upbringing. Very little of the preaching do I remember except sadly my dislike of it. I often wished I could just stop going and go out and play instead. My father used to get us to take notes of the sermons and I remember him taking our notes and giving them to the minister to read. My younger sister's notes seemed to impress them greatly which

made me feel rather jealous that they should like her notes better than mine.

There were sad times too. One morning before going to school a neighbour came and told us that three of our school friends had been drowned. I remember the shock and tears and wondering were they in heaven or in hell.

We attended two churches, one beside us and the other twelve miles away. Both ministers were very kind to my family. The minister from Dingwall used to visit us and I well remember that when we would see his car come along the road we would stop our game and see who would be first to meet him - this included the local children. We would all then pile into the good front room and sit there panting and puffing waiting for him to read God's Word and pray for us.

Suddenly, amidst this happy childhood disaster struck; my father took ill. I vividly remember the worry and fear even as a child of, 'What if Dad dies?' My father had a small grocer's business and used to go out with a grocery van to all the country villages and houses. This meant long hours so it was a frequent occurrence to see my father come home late, tired and hungry and my mother giving him his dinner at 10 o'clock at night. However, one night he did not arrive home and I remember as a

twelve-year-old going to the window with my mother to watch for the lights of his van coming up the road. I remember asking God to bring him home.

At midnight an ambulance drew up at our house, and my oldest sister got out. She had been helping my father that day with his grocery round. Dad had become ill and was taken into hospital. Three weeks later he had died. I remember the tears and sadness in the house and wondering what would happen to us all. Not once did I think of asking God for help except that first evening. Children have their own way of coping with grief and as long as things remain stable and secure they soon get over it. My mother and three older brothers provided that stability and security for me and I suspect for my younger brother and sister.

It was around the time of my father's death that my older brothers began to seek Christ. One by one I saw all my brothers and sisters converted. Two remained unconverted, myself and an older sister, but I still put it as far away from me as possible.

My younger sister and I were very close, and laughed, played and squabbled together. I always felt, indeed I knew that she was keener to be saved than I was. The day arrived inevitably when she too was saved and I thought that

perhaps we would not have the closeness that we used to have. Needless to say we became even closer, but I can see now that it was due to my sister. Her love and concern for me became stronger and many, many times she talked to me about my own salvation. Often I wished she'd just be quiet, other times she would touch a cord and I'd think, "I really must try and get saved," followed by the thought, "but I don't really want it yet."

Leaving home

By this time I had left school and was having a 'good time' as I thought in the world. I then went to work in Glasgow and lived with my older brother and sister. It was our custom to go to the neighbouring churches of our denomination in Edinburgh and Greenock when they held the Lord's Supper. I felt trapped and longed to escape from it all and live life my way. I often wonder at God's patience with me. How I made it so plain to him that I did not want him in my life and yet how he kept me from falling into open sin, although many times I came so close to it.

All too soon I was 21 years old. I came home from work to a surprise birthday dinner surrounded by presents and family.

Around this time I began to worry about

death, "What if I didn't waken up in the morning?" It didn't keep me from going to sleep but it was there. I started trying to read my Bible and praying but I found I had nothing to say to God. I'd try and repeat the prayers I'd learned but I felt as if I was saying them to nobody.

In 1970, I was married and my husband and I set up home in Inverness. Three years later we had a baby boy. You would think having a loving husband and beautiful baby would have made me so happy, but all I had was an empty, black void that desperately needed filling. I loved my husband and baby but they did not fill this empty void. Each night as I went to sleep I used to long for the empty, dark void to go away, and would hope that perhaps when I'd waken it would be gone. I would not be long awake when it would flood over me. Wasn't God good leaving it with me? He knew exactly what I needed to turn me to him.

Around this time I had to be hospitalized. I was worried and afraid. My oldest brother came to see me and was not long at my bedside when I began to weep. His concern showed in the way he prayed for me and lovingly pointed me to Christ - still I resisted. Nothing satisfied me. Looking back I was quite a difficult person to live with because of my discontentment. Many times my husband would ask me what

was wrong, but I would not tell him as I knew he would point me to Christ and I did not want that.

Time went by and one day my husband told me he thought God was calling him to be a minister. Disaster! I thought this is definitely the worst thing that has come upon me. Three of my brothers had become ministers and one sister was married to a minister, and their life-styles were not attractive to me. My husband along with his brother had their own business. I remember weeping and crying and saying to God, "You can do what you like to us but don't let Don go in for the ministry." Praise God, he did not answer that prayer. Gradually I became reconciled to the idea and thought, "I'll help him in every way I can but I won't be able to help on the spiritual side." This worried me. During all this, not once did I confide in anyone - not even my husband. I can't imagine what devastation my husband would have felt if he had known that his wife hated the idea of his going in for the ministry. God was protecting him, I am sure of that now. Many times I knew Don was worried about me and prayed for me.

Assurance of salvation

God answered these prayers. It was a Sunday night. While getting ready for a church service

I thought, "It's the minister who was used in my sister's conversion who is preaching tonight. Perhaps it will happen to me." As the minister gave out the text, *O foolish Galatians who hath bewitched you* (Gal.3:1), I thought, "Well, there is nothing there for me." However, during the sermon the minister said, "Oh friend, if I could convert you I would, but I can't. Pray, right now as you sit in your seat that the Lord would make you willing in a day of his power." There and then I said to Jesus, "Lord, you know how much I hate you and don't want you - make me want you, please change me."

I believe today that if I had looked at my watch then I would know even the minute that I was converted. I went home and all I wanted to do was go away with my Bible, but I could not as we had friends staying for the weekend. Next evening was our prayer meeting. One of the elders in his prayer said, "Lord, if a spark has been started in anyone, fan it and turn it into a blaze." Standing there listening I thought, "That's it. That's what has happened to me." I was deliriously happy. Yet I did not mention any of this to my husband.

Next morning I could not wait to get everyone out of the house and get my Bible out. How wonderful it was being with Jesus on my own! Truly the scales had fallen from my eyes and I

understood so perfectly what had previously seemed so obscure. Half way through the morning I phoned my husband to say that I had been converted. He came straight home and we spent a long time talking over what had happened to me. I can't truly describe the change it brought to everything, suffice to say that our marriage took on delights that it previously lacked. Even the trees looked greener!

The next weekend I went through to services in a neighbouring town. The same minister was to preach and I could hardly wait for it to come. I cannot remember where he was preaching from on the Friday evening but he was giving marks of those who know the Lord and I felt that I did not have one of them. I was devastated, all my new found joy had vanished. I wasn't saved after all!

I had gone through to the service with friends and on the way back in the car could not wait to speak to one of them. He truly was put right there at this particular time by God to help me. By the time we reached our destination my assurance was restored. On getting home my husband and I sat up half the night, due to me - I had so much to ask that needed answering.

Jesus is with me

Soon after this we adopted a beautiful little girl.

That too was fraught with difficulties, but what a difference, I could now go to Christ, the burden bearer.

I then needed surgery. This was a worrying time for my husband and family, but I was only filled with joy - what a difference from the previous time I was in hospital! I remember saying to the Lord, "Do with my body as you please so long as it makes me more like you." The night before going into hospital I was so filled with joy that I could not sleep. I kept telling Jesus how much I loved him, my heart was filled with praise and adoration for him. He felt so close to me, almost as if he stood by my bedside.

Although I have now been converted for over ten years, instead of my love for him growing warmer I often feel it has grown cold. Many times I pray,

Lord, to my heart bring back the springtime,
May I warm and tender be again.

He has never failed me but I have failed him many times. Often I marvel at Christ's compassion. How gently he turned me around to face him.

My husband is now in the ministry in Dundee and I feel so privileged that I am able to share in

this work with him. We are able to pray, weep and laugh together.

It makes me sad when I look back on all the years that I resisted Christ and served Satan. I often get comfort from these words in Joel 2:25: *I will restore the years which the locusts have eaten.* Also when I'm cross and irritable with the children, especially after they have been naughty, I just need to think of how patient and gentle Christ is with me when I sin. I can be so harsh with the children yet he never rebukes me harshly.

10

He Found Me - Tony*

There are lots of things that can bring people to
the brink of despair: marital stress; bereave-
ment; redundancy; unemployment when you've
tried for job after job; with bringing up teenage
children; trying to make ends meet when inflation is biting, just to mention a few reasons.

But most people would agree that having to
face up to the fact that you are suffering from an
incurable disease that is pinning you down while
you are still comparatively young can be one of
the strongest reasons for despair, specially when
there are moments of unbearable pain, and
little prospect of relief in sight.

Tony was desperate. The pain was so awful.
He had been suffering from Multiple Sclerosis
for fifteen years, and had often been in pain.
But he had never felt such pain as he had in his
legs just then. He cried out aloud, hardly knowing what he was saying, "Oh my God! Oh my
God!"

Suddenly he found himself wondering, "Who
is my God? Where is my God? Is he listening?

*This account was written by Tony's friend, Leith Samuel.

147

Can he really help? Or is he far away, quite out of reach?"

Help came all right. First, the doctors at the hospital round the corner wrapped hot towels round his legs, and he was amazed at the relief this simple procedure brought to his limbs.

For the second level of help, Tony had to wait a bit longer. Two or three weeks later he was in hospital, and we found ourselves in the next beds to one another in a ward for six, but not a distinctively MS ward. By this time Tony had begun to feel that the God he was wondering about might be found through reading the Bible. Help couldn't be far away now. Surely there would be a Bible in the locker beside his hospital bed. But there wasn't. He did not know that the Southampton hospitals are among the very few in Britain where the Gideons are not permitted to put a Gideon Bible or New Testament and Psalms beside every bed.

I heard Tony's disappointed exclamation, "There isn't a Bible in my locker!" I could hardly believe my ears! I shot up in bed.

"A Bible? Do you want a Bible?"

"Yes," he said. "Where can I buy one?"

"I'll get you a Bible," I said, and went straight off to the telephone to ring some Gideon friends who were only to pleased to come that evening with a good print New International Version

New Testament and Psalms. There was only one condition for receiving this hardback book - that Tony should read it every day. I must confess I hardly expected him to rise to that. How wrong can you be?

Five or six weeks later I had a phone call from Tony's wife. "Tony would like you to come and see him. I asked the vicar to come, and he said he would, but he didn't. Will you come?"

Delighted to be drawn in like this, I said I would be along at about three that afternoon. I went to get the car out at five to three and found the battery flat. The retired bank manager next door promptly got out his car and took me. And when I got back by bus I found he had kindly fixed his battery charger on to my flat battery! *Neighbours! Everybody needs good neighbours!* I've certainly had them, on both sides.

Tony greeted me from his bed with just one word, "Bethesda!"

That was a coded way of telling me such a lot. First, that he had been reading John's Gospel, as I had urged him to before we parted in hospital, and he had got as far as the fifth chapter at least. Second, that what happened to the cripple of whom we read in that chapter had really caught Tony's imagination. The man in the story had been ill for thirty eight years,

and was to be found every day lying with a number of other hopefuls by the old pool of Bethesda, near St. Stephen's Gate in the present walls of Jerusalem.

"You mean you would like a repeat performance?" I asked. Tony nodded.

"Well, I've been to Bethesda three times, and it's only a puddle today. You couldn't possibly get your legs in."

Naturally Tony looked a little disappointed. I went on.

"But just suppose you got your legs healed? How old are you, forty?"

"No," he replied, "only 34." I should say he looks younger now than he did then.

"Lets add 36 to 34. What does that make it?"

"70," he replied. "That's it. Three score years and ten."

By which he meant that that was all he would expect on average, in spite of the many who live so much longer these days.

"Right, if you reach 70, and finish, and don't know where you are going, what good would it be to you that your legs were healed when you were 34?"

The conversation stopped. Tony was thinking hard.

Then I went on, "Tony, God is God, and because he is God, the great Creator God, he

could heal your legs. He could heal you of anything. But I'm not at all sure it is his will to do so. We can ask him confidently to do what is best for you. But there are two things I am absolutely certain God is prepared to give you, and you may know that you have them for sure: the free gift of the forgiveness of all your sins, and the free gift of everlasting life. You may receive these two free gifts and know that you have them for keeps."

Tony's face was responsive. It was obvious that he had not banked everything on what happened to his legs. It was God himself, and God's provision for his deepest needs that he was seeking. And he wasn't prepared to turn his back on God if God didn't perform a quick miracle on his legs and heal him completely of his long-standing MS. His two boys, sharp little fellows - hyperactive according to Mum! - were in and out much of the time that we were talking. This was more important than I knew! For the seven year old doesn't want to be missing when I visit these days, and always wants to be in on the prayer at the end!

Just before I left I asked Tony how he had been getting on with his daily Bible reading. He said he had not been finding it easy to concentrate. "But," he added with great emphasis, "the more I've read, the more I've believed!'

What an encouragement for the Gideons and anybody who passes on parts of the Bible in the language of the person receiving it. *This is a trustworthy statement that deserves full acceptance, that Christ Jesus came into the world to save sinners* ... says Paul in 1 Timothy 1:15-16.

I didn't think Tony was likely to ask for the wonderful gift of the forgiveness of sins until he was fully conscious that he was a sinner in the sight of God. So the next time I went I asked him, "Tell me, do you sometimes get hopping mad with your wife because she doesn't come fast enough when you call her?"

"Oh, I do, I do," he said, with more than a little feeling. "I sometimes get so angry with her that I say things I wish I'd never said."

"So you know you're a sinner then, Tony?"

"I do," he said.

That was important. We can't expect God to meet our deepest need until we know and confess it. That was the most important thing for Tony to grasp that day in his progress towards finding, or being found by, the living God he had called out to in such despair seven or eight weeks earlier.

Next time we met we thought about the Cross of Christ, as we were getting near to Easter 1989. "Why did Jesus have to die such a cruel and awful death?" Tony asked. He was

obviously moved as we went over the familiar story found in the Gospel records, noting the following details, which some would describe as 'The Seven Words from The Cross'.

The First Word from The Cross:
As Jesus was being nailed to the cross-piece, he said, "Father, forgive them. They don't know what they are doing" (Luke 23: 33,34). Amazing grace!

The Second Word from The Cross:
When he saw his mother Mary standing there weeping, and his cousin John, son of Salome, Mary's sister, standing nearby, he said, "Dear woman, here is your son," and to that disciple, "Here is your mother" (John 19: 25-27). And the record tells us that from that time, this disciple took her into his own home. Amazing thoughtfulness in spite of his appalling pain!

The Third Word from The Cross:
Two criminals were crucified with him, one on either side. One hurled insults at him: "Aren't you the Christ? Save yourself and us," i.e. "If you are what you say you are, and I don't believe it for a moment, show it by getting yourself and us out of this lot."

But the other criminal, in spite of the physi-

cal agony he was enduring on the cross, rebuked his fellow-sufferer. "Don't you fear God," he said, "since you and I are under the same sentence of death? You and I are both being punished justly, for we are getting what our deeds deserve. But this man has done nothing wrong."

Then he said to the one on the centre cross, "Lord Jesus, remember me when you come into your kingdom."

Jesus answered him, "I tell you the truth, you (singular, not both of them) will be with me in Paradise today" (Luke 23:39-43).

Once again, what can we say but amazing grace! One gets in at the very last minute. Who was it that made it clear to him that Jesus was the Lord, that Jesus was not suffering for his own sins (but for ours) and that Jesus, this humiliated Sufferer on the cross was surely coming into a kingdom, a place of supreme power and eternal authority? Only the Spirit of God could have done that. And each of us needs such working of the Holy Spirit in our minds if the same vital truths are to dawn on us.

It is worth noting that only one of these two guilty men was saved at the last minute, so that no one need despair. It is not too late for you to come to the Lord Jesus to put your trust in him as the one who died for your sins. But the other

was not saved at the last minute, so that none should presume. And the man who says 'I'll call on him at the eleventh hour' may find he is called at ten thirty!

On the way to see Tony this particular day I had driven through the cemetery and seen my wife's grave. This had reminded me vividly how glad I am that she too is with the Lord Jesus in Paradise. As she said to me a couple of weeks before she went, "I know where I am going, and I am not afraid. But only because of what he has done for me." He had gone to hell for her, so that she might go to heaven with him.

The Central Word from The Cross:
While the Lord Jesus was hanging on the cross, at midday a terrifying darkness came over the whole land, as if the very sun was hiding its face for shame at the awful treatment being handed out to its Creator by his rebellious creatures. The creatures were crucifying their Creator! Then out of the darkness came an awful cry, "Eloi, Eloi, lama, sabachthani?" "My God, my God, why have you forsaken me?" (Matt. 27:45,46).

Do you know the answer to that awful question, that cry of desolation? I never grow tired of saying it: He was forsaken so that we might be forgiven, and never forsaken. He who knew

no sin, did no sin, entertained no sinful thought, was made a sin-offering for us (2 Cor. 5:21). Something unspeakably awful happened to him, so that something unspeakably wonderful might happen to us. As the old hymn puts it,

> There was no other good enough
> to pay the price of sin;
> He only could unlock the gate
> Of heaven and let us in.

The Fifth Word from The Cross:
As Jesus hung and suffered there, he suddenly cried out, "I am thirsty" (John 19:28). A Guild of Women always provided a jar of wine vinegar for the relief of those being crucified. He had declined it earlier lest it should dim the full horror of God-forsakenness (hell); he now accepted. He was back in the sunshine of his Father's love. They soaked a sponge in the wine vinegar, put it on a long stalk, and lifted it to his lips. And from those lips came a great shout of victory.

The Sixth Word from The Cross:
"It is finished!" Not 'I am finished,' but 'It is finished!' What was finished? The full paying of the price of sin, the price of our forgiveness (John 19:30; Hebrews 9:25-28).

The pain which he endured
Our salvation has procured,
Hallelujah! No more to pay for sin.
Jesus paid it all!

What is finished? The only bridge that reaches all the way from earth to heaven. Not a plank missing! Not one component part missing! Finished. Complete!

What is finished? The paying of the full price of a single, one way only, untransferable ticket to heaven. A ticket each of us must come to Christ for personally if we are to get to heaven when we die.

The Last Word from The Cross:
Then, to cap it all, came from the lips of the Lord Jesus the words of personal committal to the final experience in the process of dying, no longer separated from his Father by our sin, "Father, (not 'my God', but 'my Father'!) into your hands I commit my spirit" (Luke 23:44-49).

And he breathed his last on earth. His last breath till the resurrection moment when on the third day he arose again from the dead in a glorified human body, the model of that body which awaits all those, of whatever race or from whatever part of the world, who have come to him for forgiveness and the free gift of

everlasting life (Philippians 3:20,21).

"Tony," I went on, "let's imagine two more words on the cross over Christ's head: 'For men.' Now let's take the last letter off the word 'men'."

"For me," he said, deeply moved.

"Wouldn't it be wonderful," I continued, "if your wife were to turn to the Lord at the same time as you, thanking him for dying on that first Good Friday for your sins?"

"I'm an atheist," came a quick reply from the corner of the bedroom where she was working on a computer.

"You mean you haven't enough information to act on yet?" I replied, and told her how my daughter had had similar problems. "How can we know it isn't all a fairy story, Daddy?" she had asked at one of those delightfully pro-tracted bed-times! I told her how Margie had been helped by reference to that day's newspaper, which bore silent witness to the truth of Christ's death and resurrection by the date it bore - an Anno Domini date. We date our birthdays from the calendar. Jesus Christ has dated the calendar from his birthday. Why? Because he is the only person in the whole wide world to lay down his life and take it up again in resurrection power, giving many, convincing proofs that he was alive again.

Something happened. Something totally extraordinary. And every newspaper today bears witness to it, whether in Prague or Bratislava, Moscow or Budapest, Paris or London, Warsaw or Berlin, New York or Toronto. The hour may be different but the date is the same - A.D.

"I'm not going to wait for her," said Tony. "I'm going to show her the difference it makes!" And he and I expect her, a lovely person, and their two lively sons, to come to the Lord in his own good time.

Good Fridays had come, and Good Fridays had gone without leaving much impression. But this Good Friday was different, because Tony had come personally to the Lord Jesus Christ for the two wonderful free gifts, the forgiveness of all his sins, and everlasting life.

"Do I have to try to get out of bed and stand to talk to him?" Tony had asked. Lovely question, indicating his great respect for the God to whom he was now coming. I assured him that God looks on the heart. And we don't have to go to a special place to come to him.

Tony has passed from spiritual death into spiritual life, from spiritual darkness into spiritual light, from very understandable despair into vital personal trust in the living God. From being quite out of touch with God he has come into a warm personal relationship with him.

If anyone is in Christ, he is a new creation. The old has gone, the new has come! (2 Corinthians 5:17).

He still has his difficult moments, but no more despair. 'The more I read the Bible, the more I believe,' he says with relish.

I wish you could have heard Tony tell a hospital chaplain at Ashurst how he had become a Christian. And I wish you could have been with me on a recent visit to their home when he said, "Do you know, she washed my hair this morning!" As if to say, "Isn't she wonderful! She does so much for me. I can never thank her enough!"

She will be even more wonderful when she has put her trust personally in the Lord Jesus, thanking him for dying for her, asking him to take complete charge of her life. Have you done that? Have you come to him personally? There is no other way to heaven and lasting peace of mind.

When Satan tempts me to despair,
And tells me of the guilt within,
Upward I look, and see him there
Who made an end of all my sin.

Because my sinless Saviour died
My sinful soul is counted free;
For God, the Just is satisfied
To look on him and pardon me.